The Homeless

ISSUES FOR THE NINETIES

Volume 5

Editor

Craig Donnellan

Independence

Educational Publishers

Cambridge

First published by Independence
PO Box 295
Cambridge CB1 3XP

© Craig Donnellan 1995

British Library Cataloguing in Publication Data
The Homeless – (Issues for the Nineties Series)
I. Donnellan, Craig II. Series
362.5

ISBN 1 872995 59 4

Printed in Great Britain
at Leicester Printers
Leicester

Cover
The cartoon on the front cover is by
the artist, Ken Pyne

Typeset by
Martyn Lusher Artwork, Cambridge

CONTENTS

Introduction

The Homeless is the fifth volume in the series: **Issues For The Nineties**. The aim of this series is to offer up-to-date information about important issues in our world.

The Homeless examines homelessness in the United Kingdom, and the problems confronting refugees and asylum seekers around the world. The information comes from a wide variety of sources and includes:

Government reports and statistics
Newspaper reports and features
Magazine articles and surveys
Literature from lobby groups
and charitable organisations.

It is hoped that, as you read about the many aspects of the issues explored in this book, you will critically evaluate the information presented. It is important that you decide whether you are being presented with facts or opinions. Does the writer give a biased or an unbiased report? If an opinion is being expressed, do you agree with the writer?

The Homeless offers a useful starting point for those who need convenient access to information about the many issues involved. However, it is only a starting point. At the back of the book is a list of organisations which you may want to contact for further information.

*****

Homelessness in England

The facts

Level of homelessness in England

- In 1994, 127,290 households were accepted as homeless by councils in England (this figure includes about 4,630 households who were 'intentionally homeless').

- Shelter estimates that this represents 365,000 individuals.

- These figures are the tip of a very large iceberg because they only include those homeless households defined as being in 'priority need' for rehousing. This does not, for example, include the majority of single homeless people.

Thousands of single homeless people in Britain

- There are no comprehensive statistics for single homelessness nationally. In London alone Single Homelessness in London (SHIL) have estimated that there are 77,000 single homeless people.

- The 1991 Census recorded 2,674 people sleeping rough in England. The actual figure is likely to be much higher because of the difficulty in counting less visible homeless people, and those moving in and out of temporary accommodation.

- Shelter estimates that there are up to 8,600 people sleeping rough in England.

Other vulnerable groups

- Black people form a disproportionate number of those accepted as homeless by local authorities and spend longer in temporary accommodation. The London Research Centre estimates that black people represent 39% of those accepted as homeless by London authorities.

- According to a recent Government survey (1993) about half of single homeless women in bed and breakfast hotels and hostels are from black or other ethnic minority groups.

- During 1993 over 6,960 households were accepted as homeless owing to mental illness of one of the household members. This represents an increase of 65% since 1990, in the number of households accepted as homeless due to mental illness.

Homelessness is a national problem

- Shelter estimates that around 60% of rough sleepers are found outside of London.

- In 1994 nearly 77% of households accepted as homeless were outside the London area.

- Being accepted as homeless is by no means the end of the story. Many homeless families are placed in inadequate, temporary accommodation, such as bed and breakfast hotels, where they can stay for periods ranging from several months to years.

Temporary accommodation

- At the end of December 1994 there were 47,760 families living in temporary accommodation in England. This total does not include the 8,490 who were 'homeless at home' (i.e. those who remain in existing accommodation while a permanent home is found).

- The use of temporary accommodation in England has decreased by 11% since the end of Decem-

Photo: J Leighton / Shelter

Shelter nightline, a telephone advice service available 24 hours a day.

ber 1993, but it is still more than four times higher than ten years ago.

Bed and breakfast hotels

- The use of bed and breakfast hotels has decreased dramatically since its peak in 1991 when a total of 13,500 families were living in this type of accommodation.

- At the end of 1994 a total of 4,330 households were living in bed and breakfast hotels in England. Shelter estimates that this represents over 12,427 individuals.

- Despite the decline in the number of households living in bed and breakfast, around 2.2 million nights were booked in bed and breakfast accommodation by local authorities in England in 1993/94 at an estimated gross cost of £65 million.

Homelessness due to repossessions

- According to the Council of Mortgage Lenders a total of 49,210 properties were taken into possession in 1994 in the UK. This represents a decrease of 16% from 1993.

- At the end of 1994 a total of 419,890 home owners were in mortgage arrears. Of these 117,110 were more than 12 months in arrears.

- In 1994 a total of 77,681 mortgage possession orders were made against home owners in England and Wales.

- These figures show the level of misery being suffered by a large number of people.

The way forward

- Shelter recognises that the continued use of temporary accommodation is due to the shortage of affordable permanent homes.

- Shelter believes that at least 100,000 affordable permanent homes are needed each year to meet the high levels of housing need.

Shelter believes that a decent affordable home should be available to everybody as a human right.

© Shelter
March, 1995

Singled out

Young homeless people in Scotland

The following is a compilation of information and research on young homeless people in Scotland:
- In the year 1992/93, 10,400 single young people aged between 16 and 25 applied for help under the homeless persons legislation.[1]
- This is likely to be an underestimate of the true figures since many young people will not apply to district or islands councils for help because they do not believe the council can help them.
- Many district or islands councils do not consider young people to be 'in priority need'. 20 out of 56 Scottish district or islands councils in 1992 automatically considered homeless 16 and 17 year olds 'vulnerable' and therefore a priority; eight did the same for 18 year olds; two for 19–21 year olds and only one for young people aged 22–25.[2]

The Scottish Council for Single Homeless

- In 1992/93, 7% or 3,100 of total homeless applicants in Scotland were 16 or 17 years old. 17% (7,300) of applicants were aged 18–24.[1]
- SCSH research suggests around two thirds of young homeless people have experienced physical, sexual or emotional abuse.[3]
- Around 220 young people are referred to emergency hostel accommodation in Scotland each month. Only one in five can be admitted, usually because there are no free beds.[4]
- In contrast to England and Wales, the Children Act does not apply in Scotland and social work departments have no clear duty to homeless 16 and 17 year olds.

Background

Young people in Scotland have different legal rights from young people in England and Wales. In Scotland when young people reach the age of 16 they are entitled to apply for housing from the district or islands council. The council is not allowed to take any account of their age in deciding whether to give them a house (Housing [Scotland] Act 1987 Part 1).

As with any other homeless person, the council has to house young people if they are:
- homeless
- in priority need
- not intentionally homeless, and
- they don't have a local connection with another council (Housing [Scotland] Act Part 11).

There is a Code of Guidance issued by the Scottish Office on the operation of Part 2 of the 1987 Act. Councils 'must have regard to it' but the Code is not mandatory. The Code says: '... *among those who may be vulnerable for a special reason are the following which are given by way of example ... young people of 16 or 17 years old ... young people otherwise at risk ... even if they are over 17) ... young people having recently left local authority care.'* The Code also states *'The upper age limit for a "young person" is not fixed.'*

Unemployed young people aged between 18 and 25 are entitled to a lower rate of Income Support from the DSS than those aged 25 and over. 16 and 17 year olds are not entitled to Income Support unless they are in very specific circumstances or are in 'severe hardship'. In 1992, 24% of all applications from 16 and 17 year olds for Income Support due to severe hardship came from Scotland.

16 and 17 year olds have been given the guarantee of a youth training place by the Government. However, research shows that there are not sufficient YT places for everyone who wants one, and much of the training that is available is of poor quality. (*A Broken Promise* – Coalition on Young People and Social Security 1992)

If a 16 or 17 year old loses their YT place they can get a Bridging Allowance of £15 per week for a maximum of eight weeks. This figure has never been increased since it was introduced in 1988.

According to the survey of young people who contacted the Scottish Low Pay Unit, the average hourly rate paid to employed young people under 18 in 1992 was £1.64 per hour. This was effectively a drop of 9% from the previous year. More generally since then pay for low paid men is down 1% and for women down 6%.

The DSS commissioned MORI to survey 16 and 17 year olds claiming Income Support due to severe hardship. (*A survey of 16 and 17 year old applicants for severe hardship payments*, July 1991) Amongst the findings are:

- 46% had slept rough.
- 2 in 5 had lived in hostels, squats or bed and breakfast accommodation.
- 25% of the women were pregnant.
- One third had either been thrown out of the family home or had been living with relatives or friends who could no longer support them.
- One quarter said they had needed to beg, steal or sell drugs in order to survive.
- More than 75% had been unemployed for more than one week. Almost half had no money at all when they claimed. About 1 in 10 had been in care.
- 22% had been physically or sexually abused by someone in the family home or by staff at a children's home.

Not only are the Income Support rates difficult for young people, but other aspects of the social security system make it hard to get a house, or if they have a house, to furnish it. The Social Fund was introduced in 1988 to replace a system of grants. It is impossible for young people to get a deposit (as grant or loan) from the Social Fund which would help them secure accommodation. Young homeless people are very unlikely to get a grant or loan to get furniture from the DSS. Some young people have been turned down for a loan from the Social Fund because they are too poor to pay the loan back. A recent report by the DSS showed Social Fund Officers believe the Fund does not help those in the greatest need (*Working the Social Fund*, 1992).

Why are they homeless?

Young people become homeless for many different reasons. Usually there is not just one reason. There are both 'push' and 'pull' factors which lead to young people leaving home. 'Push' factors include being thrown out, family conflict, leaving care, overcrowding and poor housing conditions. 'Pull' factors include becoming more independent, looking for work, going to live with a partner. Usually leaving home is the result of a combination of factors.

A survey of young Scots with an average age of just over 19 showed that 28% had already left home (*Scottish Young Persons Survey*, Centre for Educational Sociology, Edinburgh University). 34% left to continue their education, 29% left to go to a job, 22% to get married or set up home on their own and 16% left because of problems at home. Most young people leave home successfully, but there is a correlation between leaving home in an unplanned way and becoming homeless.

For many young people the first attempt to set up home does not work. If there are problems living independently many people can return home. Of those who did leave home by age 19, 28% returned home again (*Young People In and Out of the Housing Market*, Paper 3, Jones G, SCSH/Edinburgh University).

Homelessness can result from losing a job, ending a course or breaking up with a partner. Nearly 60% of homeless young people left home because of conflict at home. For them returning home is not an option.

Many of those who become homeless may have experienced emotional, physical or sexual abuse. Many others will have spent some time in care. Recent research by SCSH and Shelter (Scotland)[4] shows that 40% of young homeless people applying for emergency accommodation had spent some time in care. Those who are forced to leave home and become homeless may well spend some time sleeping rough. The same research shows that 45% of young people in emergency hostel accommodation had slept rough previously, with the percentage much higher in urban areas. Young people leaving care are particularly at risk.

1 *Scottish Office Statistical Bulletin* HSG 1994/2
2 *Some Change – Some Chance!* Shelter (Scotland) 1993
3 *Young People In and Out of the Housing Market* 1993 SCSH/ Edinburgh University Centre for Educational Sociology
4 *No Place Called Home*, Shelter / SCSH 1994

Homelessness

Social trends

Part III of the Housing Act 1985, and its Scottish equivalent, requires local authorities to help homeless people in defined categories of 'priority need'. Essentially these are families with young children, women expecting babies and those vulnerable through old age, physical disability, mental handicap or illness. They may help others not in these categories, either by securing accommodation or by providing advice and assistance to enable them to find accommodation themselves.

A council's first responsibility is to satisfy itself that an applicant is homeless or threatened with homelessness. Once satisfied it must determine whether the applicant has a priority need. If this is the case then the council has responsibility to provide permanent accommodation. The legislation does not require councils to provide local authority accommodation in all cases, but allows them to make arrangements for homeless people to

---

The use of bed and breakfast accommodation has declined dramatically over the last two years

---

be housed by a housing association or in private accommodation.

In 1993 nearly 340 thousand households in Great Britain applied to local authorities to be accepted as homeless (Table 1 below). Around half of them were found to be in priority need. Of those households in priority need found accommodation in 1993, 60 per cent were households with children and a further 12 per cent had a pregnant household member. The proportion of households with a household member who was vulnerable because of mental illness has more than doubled since 1989, but still only accounted for 5 per cent of those

households in priority need. In Northern Ireland in 1993 around 10 thousand households applied to the Northern Ireland Housing Executive in the province to be accepted as homeless.

The most common reason for households being homeless in 1993 was that they were no longer able to live in accommodation which was currently being provided by parents, relatives or friends (Graph 1). Those homeless households found accommodation because of a breakdown in relationship with their partner accounted for just over 20 per cent of all cases in 1993 compared with only 16 per cent in 1981.

A survey carried out by Social and Community Planning Research in 1991, on behalf of the Department of the Environment, indicated that statutorily homeless households are offered permanent accommodation immediately in just under a quarter of local authorities. However, virtually all London boroughs placed

---

Table 1: Homeless households – applications and households found accommodation

		Percentages		
Great Britain	*1986*	*1989*	*1991*	*1993*
Households applying as homeless				
Total enquiries *(thousands)*	249.1	333.0	346.8	339.4
Homeless households in priority need found accommodation				
Household with dependent children	65	68	65	60
Household member pregnant	14	13	13	12
Household member vulnerable because of:				
Old age	7	6	4	5
Physical handicap	3	3	3	4
Mental illness	2	2	3	5
Other reasons[1]	9	7	11	13
All in priority need[2] *(= 100%) (thousands)*	107.7	128.7	160.7	154.1
Homeless households not in priority need found accommodation *(thousands)*	10.2	13.2	9.8	6.7
All households found accommodation *(thousands)*	117.9	142.0	170.5	160.8

[1] Includes 'homeless in emergency.'
[2] Includes actions where priority need category is not known.

Graph 1: Homeless households found accommodation by local authorities: by reason[1] for homelessness, 1993

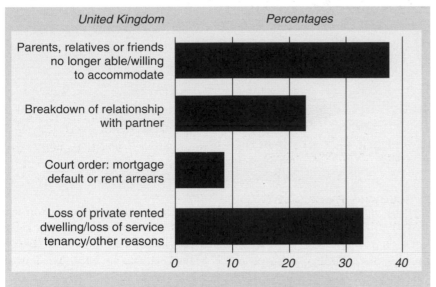

United Kingdom	Percentages
Parents, relatives or friends no longer able/willing to accommodate	
Breakdown of relationship with partner	
Court order: mortgage default or rent arrears	
Loss of private rented dwelling/loss of service tenancy/other reasons	

0   10   20   30   40

[1] Categories in Wales and Northern Ireland differ slightly from those in England so cases have been allocated to the closest English category. Data for Wales include priority cases given advice and assistance but excludes those that fall into the non-priority category.

Source: Department of the Environment; Welsh Office; The Scottish Officer; Department of the Environment, Northern Ireland

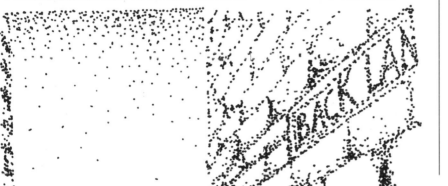

households in temporary accommodation first, compared with 70 per cent of the non-metropolitan districts. After steadily increasing up to 1992, the number of households in Great Britain who were living in temporary accommodation at the end of the year, awaiting permanent rehousing by local authorities, fell by 13 per cent in 1993, to 58 thousand (Table 2). Seventy per cent of these households were accommodated in property leased by local authorities on a short-term basis. This accommodation included dwellings such as mobile homes, privately leased dwellings and permanent accommodation used on a temporary basis. The use of bed and breakfast accommodation has declined dramatically over the last two years. It accounted for nearly one in ten households living in temporary accommodation in 1993, compared with one in five in 1991. The number of households in Great Britain living in this type of accommodation in 1993 was 5.5 thousand, the lowest figure since 1984. In 1993 around 2 thousand Northern Ireland homeless households were living in temporary accommodation; three quarters of these were living in dwellings rented from the private sector.

Social Trends 25
© Crown Copyright
1995

Table 2: Homeless households living in temporary accommodation[1]

Great Britain		Thousands		
	Bed & Breakfast	Hostels	Short life leasing	Total
1982	2.0	3.7	4.8	10.5
1983	3.0	3.6	4.5	11.1
1984	4.2	4.2	5.3	13.7
1985	5.7	5.0	6.7	17.3
1986	9.4	5.0	8.3	22.7
1987	10.6	5.7	10.5	26.8
1988	11.2	6.8	14.2	32.3
1989	12.0	8.6	19.9	40.5
1990	11.7	10.4	27.0	49.1
1991	12.9	11.7	39.7	64.3
1992	8.4	12.6	46.6	67.6
1993	5.5	12.0	41.0	58.4

1 Data are at end year and include households awaiting the outcome of homeless enquiries. Households made temporarily homeless through flooding in Wales in 1990 and 1993 are excluded.
Source: Department of the Environment; Welsh Office; Scottish Office

Child runaways sink into crime

About 98,000 under-16s take to the streets each year, losing touch with society. Glenda Cooper reports on a charity's call for action.

More than 10,000 children will run away 10 times or more before their 16th birthday, turning to crime and prostitution to survive, according to a report launched by the Children's Society today.

The report, *Running – The Risk*, reveals 98,000 children, some as young as 11, run away each year, spending months and even years on the streets where they face becoming 'non-citizens'.

'There is a danger of these children becoming so isolated that they cease to be citizens of our society,' Ian Sparks, chief executive of the Children's Society, said; 'They lose contact with all caring agencies, their education is very limited and they become invisible.'

Such children could spend large amounts of time out of society, he said. One 14 year old girl had spent three years living on the streets, with little contact with the adult world.

Nearly 90 per cent of run aways run first from home, and 70 per cent will run twice or more and return. The most common reason given was violence in the family and nearly half reported physical violence at the hands of parents or step-parents, with incidents often extreme and repeated. Bullying, mistreatment by staff (in residential care) and not being listened to were also major reasons.

Runaways, too young to claim benefit, turned to crime and prostitution to survive. More than half of those interviewed had stolen and at least one in seven had had sex for money. Their physical and mental health was poor. More than a quarter had been physically hurt and/or sexually assaulted on the streets. And nearly half who responded to questions about their welfare in the last three months had tried to harm themselves, either by slitting their wrists, taking an overdose or trying to hang themselves.

> ### 98,000 children, some as young as 11, run away each year, spending months and even years on the streets where they face becoming 'non-citizens'

The Children's Society is calling for new work involving parents, schools and social services, aimed at stopping young people running away in the first place. This includes education projects in schools to reach young people before they are driven to run away, and mediation focusing on family or residential care to resolve situations which cause children to run away for the first time.

Children who become detached from society can be helped by refuges such as the Children's Society Leeds Safe House and Porth Project, which can house them for up to 14 days.

'We need to reach young people before they become desperate,' Mr Sparks said, 'We need early intervention to help them. If we, society as a whole, made more emphasis supporting and helping parents, a lot of problems would not happen in the first place.

'And residential care is not as good as it should be. There is not enough training or resources, which is an issue for the Government.'

If the problem of young runaways was ignored, he warned, the consequences could be serious. 'These children will grow up into homeless adults detached from society. They are prime candidates to perpetuate the situation. We are looking at wasted lives.'

© *The Independent* November, 1994

When home is hell...
kids run away

'When I first got onto the streets I thought it was wicked, I thought it was fun, but later on I had a gun put to my head in Cardboard City'

The last time they counted, a hundred and fifty six thousand young people under 25 slept on the streets. We talked to several, but what Tat says here really affected us. There doesn't seem to be anything anybody can do for her.

Tat's been living on the streets for four years. So why did she run away from home?

'Well, I didn't really. My parents went to prison when I was twelve, and then I went into care in a children's home and one of the staff kept picking on me. I was only there for two weeks and then ran away and travelled around with the travellers for two years. I've been on the streets of London now for two years. Um, it's okay. You get addicted to being homeless.' But she says it's quite rough and you grow up a lot.

'You've got to get on the same level as all the older people. They say that I may look 16, but in my head I act about 20. I'm more streetwise than anything.

'There's a lot of things that you'd know about indoors that I most probably wouldn't ever know, but I know more about begging and building bashes – a bash is like a cardboard box, like a shed and you build it and live in there.'

We asked her what it's really like to beg?

'Begging? It makes me feel horrible, depressed, unwanted, and sometimes I beg and I get really dirty looks – but I don't sign on because I'm not old enough, so all I've got to do is either beg or steal. Some girls

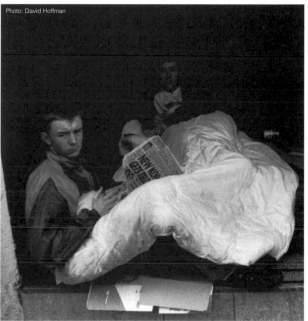

Photo: David Hoffman

around here go into prostitution, and I thought about it but I wouldn't do it, so . . . begging's okay, I suppose.'

She sleeps in a tunnel because they blocked off the doorways where she used to sleep. 'I get woken up every morning. If I don't get up when they wake me up, then they chuck water over us or spray it over us with hosepipes.'

'Who does? Security guards, sometimes workmen, sometimes the police kick you in your back . . . it makes you feel really unwanted.'

Tat comes across lots of other young homeless people in London.

'I've never trusted my family, I don't really trust anyone on the streets. The only person that I can trust is my dog'

'The youngest I met was a boy who was eight and he ran away from his parents and he was hiding in a tunnel, and I wanted him to go back home, because I've never really had proper parents, but he wouldn't. He wanted to stay with me.'

It must be incredibly dangerous for someone that young, but Tat says it gets more dangerous the older you are. 'When I first got onto the streets I thought it was wicked, I thought it was fun, but later on I had a gun put to my head in Cardboard City. I've been raped about three times and there's lots of older women that get jealous of you because you're younger and attractive, and they want to beat you up.'

We asked if she got any help from social services. 'No, they annoy me because they won't give me no money and they just say to give up my dog and then put me in a hostel which is what I don't want.'

'I think I like the streets, I think it's where I've felt most happy in a way. I get a lot of attention off all the homeless people because I'm the youngest on the Strand. There's a woman I've known for two years and I call her mum and she's about forty and really nice. But sometimes when she drinks she just turns on me and she changes.'

So is there anybody she feels she can trust?

'I've never trusted my family, I don't really trust anyone on the streets. The only person that I can trust is my dog.' © *The Guardian* *October, 1994*

7

Switching on to the young

Government must look beyond myths about the homeless and tackle the issues

After two years of talking to social service departments, housing departments, voluntary agencies and young homeless people, we have decided that a series of myths are largely responsible for young people falling through the safety net. These myths clearly influence how the 1991 Children Act for homeless 16 and 17 year olds is being implemented.

Thus, according to myth, 'The Children Act only covers children up to 16,' 'All social services can do is offer children's home accommodation,' and 'homelessness is purely a housing issue.' These reflect a lack of understanding among professionals about their responsibilities under the Act and a lack of awareness about the reality. There is little recognition of the vulnerability of homeless 16 and 17 year olds. As one social worker observed, 'Social workers see homelessness as a housing problem, so they do not see why they should be phoning around for accommodation.'

As a result, many young people are passed between housing and social services departments with neither accepting responsibility. Another social worker admitted: 'We do fob young homeless people off to housing, and hope they sort them out.'

This can partly be explained by the different legislative frameworks they operate under, professional hostilities and a lack of clear procedure. The young homeless are a low priority for both agencies and when myths are combined with widely held negative attitudes and stereotypes, the young homeless are often denied the necessary services, are 'blamed' for their homelessness or seen as 'trying it on'.

Then there is the myth that young people leave home on a whim

Jacqui McCluskey and Helen Kay

or become homeless as an easy way into local authority housing. The reality is that most young people who become homeless are either thrown out or forced to leave for their own safety.

In addition, many are leaving residential care, find it difficult to obtain affordable housing, and suffer from a lack of employment opportunities, reduced benefit and a lack of support services. Another myth used by many social services departments is that if they provide a good service they will be swamped.

> **Many young people are passed between housing and social services departments with neither accepting responsibility**

Myths do not exist in isolation. When combined with a lack of resources, they are a powerful force and often provide, on the surface, viable reasons for not providing services. 'We may well place young people in accommodation that is not well suited. We may identify their special needs, but where they go is determined by what is available, says the social worker.

It is important to recognise the financial constraints local authorities operate under and to acknowledge that the Act was underfunded. However, a lack of resources cannot excuse inaction.

A number of authorities are challenging the myths. Clearly, the Government should encourage such work. Instead, it adds to the myth creation. For example, the 1988 social security changes were based on the myth that providing benefit would encourage young people to leave home. In fact, homeless 16 and 17 year olds find it difficult to survive on current benefit levels, and the system works against them.

The influence of myths in formulating policy can be seen in the Government's current homelessness review. They have proposed changes to the law because they believe certain groups (such as single parents and young people who leave home too early) are queue jumping and abusing the system, while more deserving people are being penalised.

These myths are so embedded in our view of young homeless people that they not only influence popular perceptions but also every level of policy and practice in relation to this group. And so the search for solutions is avoided.

Instead of encouraging myths, the Government should address the real issues like the lack of affordable accommodation, high youth unemployment, lack of youth training and restoring benefit levels. A solution would be more likely if we had a Government which, in creating policy, looked beyond myths and tackled root causes.

● The above is based on *Breaking the Spiral* by Jacqui McCluskey, research manager, and Helen Kay, campaigner, which was funded by the Nuffield Foundation. Details from CHAR, which works with the young homeless. See page 39 for address details.

Charity for the homeless invents luncheon voucher for beggars

Beggars could soon receive plastic vouchers from passers-by enabling them to buy food and toiletries but not alcohol.

The vouchers, of varying values, could be exchanged in shops and hostels and are seen as a way of cracking down on drunken and aggressive vagrants. The increasing number of homeless people on the streets of Britain's city centres has led the charity Crisis to look at new ways of tackling the problem of begging. 'People often have a problem with giving. A scheme like this could let them feel more confident about where and who they give their money to, knowing that it can only be spent on certain things,' a Crisis spokesman said.

The scheme is initially being considered for Manchester, where local businesses, concerned about the effect vagrancy has on their trade, are working with charities to find a solution. Central to the proposals is an all-night café that would provide shelter, food and medical care during the night for those who cannot or will not take up hostel places.

The eventual aim is to persuade the homeless to leave the streets, with the café being used as a gateway to a network of other services. 'Ultimately the aim of the scheme is to get in touch with people who are not making use of the services available to them,' Liam Black, regional director of Crisis, said. 'There are a lot of people with, for

The vouchers, of varying values, could be exchanged in shops and hostels

By Kathryn Knight

example, mental health problems, who often seem beyond our reach. We want to create somewhere where people can pass through, have something to eat and get medical advice. Hopefully we would gain their trust, find out exactly why they are

sleeping rough, and then see if we can do anything to help.'

The plastic card, currently subject to discussions between charities and the Manchester Chamber of Commerce, is seen as way of combating the aggressive begging tactics of a minority of homeless people. Crisis has identified a possible city centre site for the café and hopes that, with funding from local businesses, it will be open early next year.

A spokesman for the Chamber of Commerce said: 'Although the problem of aggressive or violent begging requires a strong law and order approach, draconian measures are wholly unsuitable. We hope this two-pronged approach will help to alleviate a problem which is affecting most sectors of the city centre.'

Lifesearch, a Manchester agency that works with the homeless, welcomed the idea of the all-night café, but said the introduction of a card system could potentially be demeaning for the homeless. A spokesman said: 'If people are willing to give money then they are not stipulating what they want it to be spent on.'

More than eight in ten people think the Government is spending too little on housing for the homeless, according to a Gallup poll published today on behalf of Shelter.

No chance!

Though reaction to people begging on the street is varied, few like the sight. But has anyone asked those who beg whether they like it? Rhonda Siddall examines the bleak reality in the light of the findings of a new report

Dave is 25 and had to beg in order to stay alive when he left care. 'I slept rough in Aberdeen docks and needed money for food. I am a diabetic and I had to eat,' he says. Alone and destitute, Dave had no choice but to rely on the pity of passers-by, who might throw him enough change for a bite to eat.

He has lived in 12 children's homes. When he left care aged 17 he tried to live with his birth mother. It did not work out and he ended up sleeping rough, first in Scotland then in London, where he sought work.

Dave's story has a happy ending. He is about to move in to a flat provided by a local housing association and is hopeful about finding a job. Jane has not been so lucky.

Like Dave, she is a care leaver who begs on London streets. Jane, 23, grew up in a children's home and was then unsuccessfully placed in three foster homes. 'Two were born-again Christians. They called me the Devil's daughter,' says Jane. As her parents are unwilling to take her back she lives in a West End short-term

hostel, supporting herself through casual work and begging, which she hates.

Begging is a risky business. Dave was hit in the face after approaching someone for money. While Jane was living on the streets she was physically abused and sexually harassed. 'I was kicked down stairs by some guy who had been in the pub. Once I woke up in the Strand and found a man trying to crawl under my blanket. I ended up on remand for hitting a guy who was trying to pull my knickers down.'

Though not all care leavers need to beg to survive, a recent study by the homelessness charity, Crisis, suggests that a high proportion of people who beg are care leavers. Of 145 people who were or had been

begging in central London, Crisis discovered most of them had had disrupted childhoods: nearly half had been in care and a quarter slept rough before they were 16. It found that 37 per cent of the sample had lived in children's homes, 10 per cent had been in special children's homes and 19 per cent in foster care.

'It was not surprising to find that nearly half the people we interviewed had been in care because other charities have published similar results,' says Alison Murdoch, author of the Crisis study. 'But it is a shocking finding. There needs to be a serious look into the care system and how it assists care leavers who move into independent living. Something is going seriously wrong.' Begging is an offence under the 1824 Vagrancy Act, which defines beggars as: 'Every person wandering abroad, or placing

himself or herself in any public place, street, highway, court or passage, to beg or gather alms.' People who beg can be arrested for feigning poverty to obtain money (1968 Theft Act) or for disorderly and threatening behaviour (the 1968 Public Order Act).

Last May, Prime Minister John Major described beggars as an 'eyesore' that was unnecessary and urged the public, police and courts to use the full force of the law against any beggars they encountered. Yet Crisis's study found that almost 80 per cent of those who beg were homeless. Many of the young people interviewed began begging due to the 1988 abolition of income support for most under 18 year olds. Money raised by begging was mostly spent on food, but 64 per cent spent it on tobacco, 47 per cent on alcohol and 26 per cent on drugs.

The fact that many of the beggars interviewed by the Crisis team were care leavers suggests that society is failing vulnerable young people. The Crisis report found that many beggars in trouble with the police had mental and physical health problems and, like Jane, were addicted to drink. 'You try to live like this without drinking – you're too nervous to sleep. I use it to pass the time, to forget, to not think about problems,' says Jane.

Paul Robertson, director of First Key, the national leaving care advisory service, says little work has been done to establish exactly why and how care leavers fall through society's safety net. 'We know some of the risk factors,' says Robertson. 'There are issues around benefit levels and the difficulty of finding secure, affordable housing. But we also know that being in care can be a risk factor if the quality of support given in terms of developing life skills for independence is questionable.' Amanda Croome, project co-ordinator of Lifeshare, puts it more succinctly. 'If income support was reintroduced for under 18s and more secure, affordable accommodation was available, many young, jobless care leavers would not have to resort to begging on the streets. And if social services departments were more willing to extend support to

---

Monitoring care leavers would alert local authorities to the nightmare of begging on the streets and put more pressure on them to make adequate provision

---

care leavers after they cease to be responsible for them, there would be less need for charities like ourselves to support young homeless people.' Lifeshare works on the streets, organising soup and tea for homeless people in Manchester. It also operates as an advisory service, helping people get a bed for the night. Croome says that many of the young people it works with are care leavers. And begging isn't the only method homeless care leavers resort to in order to survive.

One woman who ran away from care when she was 17 had no money and was not receiving benefits. So she turned to prostitution. 'One night she was attacked by a punter. We got her into a temporary hostel, but she was attacked again the next day when she decided to beg rather than work as a prostitute,' says Croome.

It is startling to encounter begging in a developed country. When confronted by a beggar it is easier to believe that begging is unnecessary and walk away, leaving him or her empty-handed. That way the more fortunate among us are not forced to acknowledge how relatively wealthy we are.

© Community Care
13–19 October, 1994

The Crisis Report's findings

Crisis interviewed 145 people who had experience of begging in central London. The interviews took place between October and December 1993, on the streets (30), in day centres and advice centres (82), and in hostels (33).

- Begging and homelessness: There is a clear link between begging and homelessness. Almost 80 per cent of respondents were homeless the previous night; 30 per cent slept rough, and the remainder stayed in temporary accommodation.
- Homelessness was not a chosen way of life: Four out of five had previously had a home – the loss of a partner was the most common reason for losing that home. All but two wanted a home.
- Most found it difficult to start begging: more than three-quarters of those interviewed found it humiliating to beg. Daily takings averaged £10 to £20; 8 per cent were receiving benefits. The most common reason given for begging was to top up benefits to buy food.
- Mental health problems: 17 per cent had been in a psychiatric hospital and one third had a history of mental health problems.
- Substance abuse: One third had a substance abuse problem, most commonly alcohol.
- Police: One in two had been arrested; 78 per cent had been moved on by police.
- Recommendations: Changes to the benefit system, improved access to emergency and long-term housing, regional strategies to tackle homelessness, extended daytime services for homeless people, and repeal of the Vagrancy Act.

This Crisis Report refutes the view that begging is unnecessary and unacceptable.

Are you 16 or 17 and homeless?

You might be entitled to this help under the Children Act.

Who from? Social Services? You must be joking. I want to get as far away from Social Services as possible. I'm not staying in a children's home.

That's OK. Social Services have to ask what you want and can help with hostels, supported lodgings or your own flat. Don't be put off asking for help because it's Social Services.

But I haven't been in care.

It doesn't matter. Under Section 17 they have a duty to help you if you are in need, and to provide accommodation under Section 20(3), if you are homeless, 16 or 17 and are a 'child in need' whose welfare is likely to be seriously prejudiced.

What does that mean?

If your emotional, physical or intellectual development is likely to be affected by your situation. Being homeless is bad for your health in lots of ways – you may not be able to sleep or eat well or get on with your life properly. Many people become homeless because of abuse or violence or being thrown out of home – in all of these cases you are 'in need.'

I was in care when I was young for a while but returned home – do I come under this part of the Act?

Yes, Section 20 is for anyone who needs help and is under 18.

I was in care after my 16th birthday – do I come under this part of the Act?

Yes, if you are under 18. You can also get help from social services under Section 24 of the Act until you are 21.

Confused?

Get an adult you trust or an advice worker to help you. Don't forget, if you are homeless you are probably a child in need.

Housing Campaign for Single People

OK – so how do I get help under Section 20 of the Act?

A step by step guide

1 If possible
Get help or advice before going to Social Services. Try to get an adult you trust to go with you.

2 At Social Services
Ask to see a social worker, if possible one with responsibility for your age group.

Don't be put off by the first person that you meet – remember that you have a right to a proper interview.

Ask for a child in need assessment under Section 20(3) of the Children Act.

At first you might not get an interview. Lots of social workers don't know about this part of the Act, but you do – so don't give up.

3 Your child in need interview
Explain to the social worker as much as possible about your situation or as much as you feel able.
Throughout your interview:
- Remember that you have a right to be heard.
- Remember that what you say should be believed.
- Remember that you can be helped without your parents agreeing – Social Services don't have to contact your parents if you don't want them to. Sorting things out

with your family so you can go back isn't their only duty to you – if you can't return home or don't want contact with your family, be clear about this and don't be pressured into doing something you don't want to.

4 Ask for a copy of your assessment in writing. Why?
It might help you make sure that you get the right service. Some Social Services might try and say you're not a child in need because they don't have much money – if you ask them to write down why they think you're not in need, then you can challenge them properly.

5 So you're a child in need. What now?
Getting somewhere to live: Make sure you tell them clearly what you want – a hostel place for a while or your own flat.

What if I'm offered a children's home or nothing?
- If this is OK for a while, then fine.
- If not, then tell Social Services it's not what you want – you want more independence.
- Social services have a duty to draw up a plan explaining how you are going to be prepared for independence. Get an advice worker to help you tell them what you want included.

Want your own council flat?
- You may have a right to this from the housing department – get an advice worker to help you ask for this.
- Social Services can also ask the housing department for your own place under the Children Act (Section 27) – ask them to sort this out for you.
- Get an advice worker to help you go through what you need – supported hostels, bed and breakfast, supported landladies etc.

6 What about support?

What does support mean?

It can mean a bit of help sorting your bills out, helping you budget your money, or helping you deal with any problems you might have.

What sort of support do you want?

Get an advice worker to help you decide what is best for you.

7 But I don't want a social worker so what's the point?

Fine – Social Services can ask a range of people to help you apart from social workers. If in doubt, ask an advice worker to help you sort out the best people for you.

What if I'm not listened to?

What if I don't get any help from social services?

Get an advice worker to help you make a complaint.

Is it all worth it?

Yes, in the end you should get the help you need.

Remember – if in doubt – get help. It will make it much easier.

Don't give up!

Characteristics associated with homelessness

The data available for 1993 in many respects confirm what is already known about the homeless. By and large such persons are drawn from those sectors of the population which could be labelled 'disadvantaged', whether one defines disadvantage in terms of housing, educational level, work opportunities and employment history, income or stability in networks of social and familial support. We cannot emphasise enough that those who become homeless are often people who already experience high risks of social marginalisation. To the extent that this is the case, homelessness is preventable.

While data deficiencies limit our capacity to analyse trends over time, the available information highlights the following trends:

● The age of people identified as homeless is falling. The modal age group is in the 30-40 decade but those aged 20 years and younger constitute a sizeable and growing proportion of persons known or estimated to be homeless.

● The number of women appearing in the homelessness statistics is growing. Moreover, the indications are that women seeking help as homeless are in different circumstances to men. Substantial proportions of these women have children and, where statistics are available, it is indicated that the average age of homeless women is lower than that of men. Three particular points should be noted in this regard. First, the vulnerability of lone parent families, the vast majority of which are headed by women, to homelessness is increasingly being indicated. Secondly, these women are often fleeing physical and/or sexual abuse within their homes. Thirdly, there are indications that existing services are better oriented to fulfilling the needs of homeless individuals as compared to those with families. Singular models of service provision are clearly no longer justifiable.

● Population dislocations occasioned by war, political unrest or poverty in countries outside the Union are placing increased pressure on the accommodation supply. The national correspondents of Germany, Greece and Italy make specific reference to such problems in their reports. In addition, the evidence available suggests some differences between homeless nationals and those from outside the Union.

● Ill-health is closely linked to homelessness. Although we still lack information on the specific linkages, evidence is increasingly becoming available that homelessness and ill-health often go together. In Spain, for example, one in three homeless people have serious health problems; a minimum of 39% of those surveyed in Italy in 1992 as 'homeless' had some form of health problem. Health policies and provision, whether in relation to access, the quality and duration of care and discharge or deinstitutionalisation procedures, are especially crucial in affecting the extent of homelessness.

● Homeless people are more likely to be unemployed than employed. Moreover, irregular employment histories are common. Given this, the state income maintenance system, where and if it is available to homeless people, tends to be their single most important source of income.

● Below-average levels of education are also commonly associated with homelessness. Although the information available is still insufficient, sizeable proportions of those enumerated as homeless have achieved only primary level education.

● The accommodation histories of homeless people where available indicate that sleeping rough and living in insecure accommodation are among the most significant patterns. Moreover, it is becoming increasingly evident that the sleeping and living patterns of those without a home are far from static, with periods of sleeping rough interspersed with stays in temporary accommodation. However, the diversity of living patterns of homeless people must be emphasised.

●The above is an extract from 'The right to a home, the right to a future' by Mary Daly – published by FEANTSA. See page 39 for address details.

Left out in the cold

The number of women sleeping rough is rising. Anna Moore reports.

Like almost half of Britain's homeless women, Rebecca was running away from abuse. Her earliest memories are of her father 'playing' with her, touching, interfering, then raping her. She ran away at 14 to spend five years in children's homes and hostels, in parks, on streets. Half Mexican, half Jewish, Rebecca is tiny – 20 years old, but looks barely 16, 'I'd escaped one man, but then there were all the others. Homeless men, businessmen, pimps trying to get me on the game. And I couldn't go home.'

The lack of available help for homeless women is enough to keep most of them on friend's floors, in abusive relationships or crummy B&Bs. Homelessness charity Centrepoint has recorded a recent increase in women sleeping rough – particularly in the youngest age bracket – but the majority of London's 2,000 beds in direct access hostels are still reserved for men. Only 378 are in women-only accommodation. 'Sometimes I'd be the only woman in a hostel of 20 older men,' says Rebecca. 'As soon as I walked in, I could feel their eyes turning. The only chance homeless men have is with other homeless women, so they'll always try it on.'

One night, Rebecca agreed to go for a drink with an ex-serviceman from her hostel. On the way back, he raped her in a doorway. Rebecca never returned to the hostel, never reported it. 'I didn't cry or anything. Afterwards, I just ran around the streets thinking "now I've got to find somewhere else to stay". I was used to bad things happening so my reactions were probably different to most people's. If I was a respectable young woman raped by some homeless person, of course I'd have gone for help. But if you're homeless, you're expected to be a tart. And going to the police is not the done thing. A lot of homeless people are breaking the law anyway – begging, prostitution, nicking stuff. The police are enemies.'

> **Nearly 40 per cent of people who beg had been sexually harassed on the street, most of them repeatedly**

Rebecca stopped going to hostels, and refused to 'pair off' with a man for protection. If women teamed up and slept together they'd soon be known as lesbians – not a name easy to live down on the street. The best place Rebecca found was a north London cemetery, all to herself. The gates were shut at dusk, but she was small enough to crawl under them. 'I felt safe because I was locked in. There was no light or shelter. No one else would think of going there.'

Last October, a Crisis report revealed that nearly 40 per cent of people who beg had been sexually harassed on the street, most of them repeatedly. The report's author, Alison Murdoch, found that women were proportionally far more vulnerable, particularly the smallest and youngest.

The harassment wasn't just from other homeless people. Murdoch noticed 'a general assumption amongst the public that women would have sex for money'.

Anita, 21, who sells *The Big Issue* in the middle of the Square Mile, can attest to this. 'Perfectly respectable looking men sidle up to me and ask, "do you perform sexual favours of any kind?" or offer to take me round Lincoln's Inn Fields for a tenner. One guy offered me luxury accommodation in Bournemouth if I went to work for him as a masseur. I was a bit stunned at first, but now I know they're all just sad men, and I tell them where to go.'

Eric Brown, project worker at Centrepoint's mixed 12-bed hostel in Soho, has seen women cope in many ways. Many pair off. 'There's a 17 year old who comes in with her boyfriend. We're pretty sure he beats her about, but she somehow feels 'safer' with him. Almost as if she's agreed to be abused by one man, to save being abused by many.'

Another young woman has a habit of spitting an invisible circle around her, making it clear no one should cross it. Another wears vicious rings and grows long, sharp nails.

'As hostel workers, all we can do is try hard to make women feel as safe and welcome as possible,' Eric says. This establishes relationships of trust with those who come in. The building is also important. Too many shelters are designed like rabbit warrens, with rooms hidden round corners, at the end of dark corridors. But even Centrepoint, as cosy and as vigilant as a hostel can be, doesn't always feel cosy enough.

'No matter what we do, there are women who won't come,' Eric says. 'They still feel safer sleeping on the street than inside a building with people they don't know.'

Nor can the police offer enough support. Alison Murdoch found most women wary of reporting problems. Many are on the run, already on the wrong side of the law, and even begging is illegal. 'The police were generally seen as people who might "pick you up", not people to turn to for help.'

Sgt Susan Hellewell of the Charing Cross Homeless Unit admits that women can be reluctant to come forward. 'They have a code whereby they don't grass. Even those who have been very badly treated often won't co-operate with us, partly for fear of reprisals.'

Hellewell maintains that the unit, set up 18 months ago, has begun to improve the relationship between police and West End homeless, allowing some women to report cases of rape and harassment. 'We treat each incident very seriously and all victims with the utmost respect.' Recently, a member of her team saw a member of the public unzip a 21 year old woman's sleeping bag on Charing Cross Road, reach in and 'have a good feel.' He was arrested, convicted of indecent assault and will be sentenced on New year's Eve. But most incidents pass without witnesses.

'It's very difficult to bring about a successful prosecution,' says Hellewell. 'Many of these women are what we call 'inadequate' – poor backgrounds, low education, few social skills. We do our best but they still have to stand up in court and be cross examined. We can't hold their hand. They can be ripped apart by barristers.'

Joanna Wade, lawyer and trustee at Crisis, believes this is why legal action is rarely taken. 'The law isn't very helpful to any woman, but it's far worse if the woman's homeless. People think there is something 'other' about them – something wrong with them. There are enormous problems with credibility.'

Protection for Rebecca came when she was caught shoplifting and placed for a year in a hostel for women offenders, staffed by women. 'It was the best thing that happened to me – the most secure place I'd ever been. Most women there had been sexually abused and the workers were trained to deal with it.'

For 50 other street women, the high point of the year falls between December 23 and 30 when Crisis opens its women-only 'Open Christmas' shelter. For this week, the women, at a secret location, are pampered by hairdressers, beauticians, aromatherapy masseurs.

One woman at the last Open Christmas had just broken out of a porn ring. 'For women with appalling histories of violence and abuse, it's the first time they've been touched sensitively for years,' says Murdoch. 'The traditional stigmatised 'bag ladies' unwind and come out of themselves. You realise that they've made themselves unapproachable just to be safe.'

As yet, there are no women's day centres for the remaining 51 weeks of the year, though two are planned by Barnardos and the Church Army.

As for Rebecca, she started a magazine at her women's hostel, rekindling her flair for writing and is now at university studying English. She has been housed in a third floor, one-bedroomed flat. 'When I was homeless and dirty, I didn't want to hold my head up high. I looked vulnerable. Now I've got things to be proud of. I still get the occasional "gissakiss darling", but that's not too bad. Now I walk away from it. I just go home.'

● *The names of the homeless women in this article have been changed.*

Sleep rough and help the homeless worldwide

By Tessa Swithinbank

Sleep out in a home-made shelter for just one night and you can help to improve the housing conditions of people living in developing countries.

Landgrab is a fund-raising event organised by Homeless International (HI), a charity working in conjunction with development organisations around the world.

HI is interested in developing long term solutions to the problems of homelessness. The critical factors, the charity argues, are self-help, finance, the creation and communication of information, and the support of local community groups, particularly those that enhance the role of women. In Andhra Pradesh, India, HI is putting these ideals into practice, helping 1,000 poor families to obtain loans so they can build permanent and safe housing.

Anyone can join in a Landgrab. All you need to do is find a site, build a shelter from waste materials, get yourself sponsored and sleep in the construction over the night of June 24-25.

For further information, contact Homeless International, 5 The Butts, Coventry CVI 3GH, Tel: (01203) 632802

Preventing homelessness, campaigning for change

Information from Shelter

Homelessness doesn't just mean sleeping on the streets. It includes people living in temporary accommodation, poor or overcrowded conditions, or under threat of repossession. Shelter defines all these people as being in housing need since they do not have decent, secure and affordable homes.

Although in England the number of households accepted as homeless by councils fell in 1993 by 5–7 per cent, Shelter believes that these 139,790 households (approximately 401,000 people) represent just the tip of a very large iceberg. These figures do not include single people or those not considered to be in 'priority need.' 'Priority need' includes families with children, preg-nant women, people with disabilities and other 'vulnerable' people.

Shelter estimates that every day in 1993, an average of 160 family homes were repossessed in the UK, and that each day in England alone an average of:

- 380 families were accepted as officially homeless.
- 5,000 families were struggling to cope with life in bed and breakfast hotels.
- 50,000 families were in other temporary accommodation.
- Up to 8,600 people slept rough.

Confronted by homelessness on such a scale, the need for Shelter's work is greater than ever before.

Shelter services

Shelter's national network of Housing Aid Centres (HACs) provides advice and information on housing rights to thousands of families and individuals. And our London Nightline telephone service offers emergency assistance every night of the year and round the clock on holidays and weekends.

Ken Pyne

In 1993/94

- 39,298 households contacted Shelter's Housing Aid Centres. We helped more than 52 per cent of them directly, and provided useful information to the rest.
- Nightline answered 24,805 calls and found emergency accommodation for 3,559 people.

Christmas crisis

In the early hours of Christmas morning, a couple from Haringey, north London, called Nightline in utter despair. On the street, with two small children, they had nowhere to go. Nightline contacted the local authority's out-of-hours homeless persons' unit immediately. As a result of our swift action, the council provided the young family with accommodation for the rest of the night and promised to look into their case.

Shelter projects

Working alongside many statutory and voluntary groups, Shelter continues to support effective, practical projects tackling local housing problems throughout the country.

Once initial research has identified and assessed specific needs, Shelter provides the finance and management skills to help local groups get such projects off the ground.

Advice Lincs

Homelessness in rural areas is increasing even faster than in cities. For people in remote areas without their own phone or transport, getting advice can be almost impossible. In 1990 Shelter helped set up Advice Lincs – a free telephone service offering confidential, impartial advice for people in Lincolnshire. The service refers callers with housing problems to the local Shelter Housing Aid Centre and last year took almost 5,000 calls.

Merseyside Young Persons' Project

The Merseyside Young Persons' Project, launched in 1990, provides young people with specialist housing advice and information, offers practical solutions to their housing problems, and equips them with a better understanding of the housing system.

In 1993/94, the project started work on an education pack for teachers, aimed at preventing young people from becoming homeless. And, by advising and assisting local agencies, it will improve and increase housing choices for young people throughout Merseyside.

Shelter campaigns
Shelter is unique in combining campaigning for long-term change with the provision of practical services. By making the public more aware of the issues surrounding homelessness and by giving politicians, businesses and housing experts opportunities to explore solutions, Shelter succeeds in getting achievable policies put into practice.

100,000 Homes campaign
Shelter has proposed a five-year programme to double council and housing association housing by creating 100,000 new homes a year. In anticipation of the 1994 Budget, Shelter submitted a package of measures to increase investment in housing, create jobs and prevent repossession. Shelter organised two major conferences, bringing together representatives from construction firms, economists, housing professionals and journalists to look at the role of housing in economic recovery.

Home Truths campaign
In January 1994, the Government proposed sweeping changes to homelessness legislation. A homeless person with accommodation, no matter how temporary, would no longer be eligible for help. And families would only have access to a permanent home via council waiting lists. Shelter launched the biggest campaign in its history and a record 10,000 responses were made. The Government has withdrawn some of its proposals but the most serious remain. The campaign goes on.

Fight to survive driven by fear and loneliness

By Glenda Cooper

Emma was 13 and unhappy at home when she ran away the first time, establishing a pattern of running away and being brought back home.

'I was frightened and very vulnerable at 13, not knowing how to survive,' she said. 'I was really not in society at all, but in my own little world. It felt like walking down a dark tunnel with a light at the end and trying to reach out for it but not getting anywhere.' She dropped out of education even though the school, and one teacher in particular, had been understanding: 'I was too busy worrying where I was going to go next, where I was going to get food from to go to school.' To buy food she turned to prostitution. 'You can't get social security until you're 16. There was no way I could get money so I did prostitution. I saw I could make quite a bit of money and it was an easy option.' She met few people on the streets – children are well-hidden, she says, so that adults cannot find them.

'I felt very alone, I can't describe it in words. This went on for a few weeks or months until I rang the Samaritans.' They told her about the Children's Society project with runaways in Leeds, called the Leeds Safe House, where she met children of her own age in a similar situation. After staying there she agreed to talk to the local authority.

Social services gave her a social worker and put her in foster care but she did not want anyone to know where she was and ran away again.

'I ended up meeting people and kipping on the floor of a house, moving constantly. At first it seemed weird – I didn't know where I was going next but I got used to living like that.' She went back to the refuge, which continued to support her: 'They were fighting my case, making plans ahead for me, finding somewhere safe.' The support of the workers helped her to survive. She now lives in a flat with her boyfriend and is picking up her education after a four-year gap.

'I'm going to make a go of it. I'm settled where I'm living now,' she said, 'I'm at college doing a diploma so I can work with young people. I want to use my experience in a positive way.' Emma added: 'Local authorities should be giving support to children, listening and trying to understand. I don't really regret running away but I think the local authority should have worked with my family as well, as my family couldn't handle it. A lot of things need to be changed.'

Moving on with the times

The untouchables: a family who finds there's no room anywhere

By Michael Simmons

Until late 1992, Martin Lawrence was self-employed, running his own agency in the Midlands. But then his business collapsed and he and his family have been on the move, technically homeless, ever since.

His wife was expecting their third child the day the repossession order came through. In fact, the baby was born a fortnight later 200 miles away in Brighton. By the time the child was a month old, the family had spent 10 days living in the family car. Many more such days were to follow.

After the south coast, Martin headed for Inverness. He says that, apart from a bag of chips for the two older children, none of them ate for three days. The local authority arranged bed and breakfast for one night but then gave the family £75 to get them off its hands. 'I needed money so badly I took it,' Martin recalls.

They headed south along the Scottish coast. At the next town, police picked them up as they prepared to spend a night in the local railway station waiting room and took them to a bed and breakfast. 'There were no carpets,' says Martin, 'the linen was stained, there were used sanitary towels in the bathroom and they wouldn't let us out of our room. It was as if we had a disease, but we stayed for three months.'

But then the council decided they were 'intentionally homeless' and suggested they return home to the Midlands. In Martin's view: 'They didn't look for ways to house us, but for ways not to.'

Two more weeks on the road. Car parks were 'good' places to stop as they had toilet facilities. On reaching the Home Counties, a local council gave them B and B for one night, but after officials rang their last Scottish contact they were told to move on.

East Anglia proved marginally more hospitable. Although the first town refused to help, the second, a dozen miles up the coast, gave them a 'crisis' loan which paid for some respite in a caravan, and for bread and margarine and lemonade for the two older children. Most importantly, it also gave them access to a 15-room B and B house, an address from which they can claim benefit.

All five are now spending most of every day in one room, the parents in a double bed, the two older children in a bunk bed, and the baby on a mattress on the floor. Each of the other 14 rooms is occupied by a 'family unit'. The car has gone for scrap.

But Martin's flair for ideas has not deserted him. Tired by the way local authorities interpret the regulations, angered that so many of them 'freely' (his word) break the law by avoiding or refusing assistance, and deeply depressed that homelessness has reached epidemic proportions, he wants to set up a non-profit-making trust called Charity Begins With A Home.

He has written to a host of household names – from Prince Charles to Richard Branson – asking them to read twice through his plans and then give him what help they can. 'The biggest problem,' he says, 'is getting people to listen.'

The trust, unencumbered by the restrictions on registered charities has several aims: to provide accommodation by converting redundant buildings, to offer rehabilitation for those who have suffered through homelessness, to increase public awareness, and break down barriers between the housed and the homeless. 'All that stands in the way of relieving an appalling situation,' Martin writes, 'is getting the backing of influential people. It needs people like you to help people like me.'

● *Further information from: The Secretary, CBWH Trust, 84 St George's Road, Great Yarmouth.*

© *The Guardian*
May, 1994

Photo: Philip Wolmuth/Panos Pictures

Doorway to a new life

For many years Chris Kitch lived rough on the streets; today, she is preparing to do a master's degree. She tells Linda Joffee about her struggle to return to society

By Linda Joffee

We have all seen them: dirty, poorly clad figures crumpled in doorways or, weighed down by their carrier bags, shuffling aimlessly; undeniably human yet, in reality, a species apart. Of all the citizenry of the street, the 'bag lady' is the most abject, pathetic and abused.

Chris Kitch was one of those blank-eyed heaps of rags and bags, invariably high on drugs or booze. For 32 years, until the age of 49, she lived in that netherworld of the homeless alcoholic and drug addict, where bottles are smashed on heads to settle scores, rapes are commonplace and a principal daily occupation is rummaging in dustbins.

But not only did Chris Kitch survive; she recently graduated with a BA hons in English literature and women's studies from North London University and has been accepted at Oxford Brookes University to do a Master's degree, beginning next autumn. Hers is a tale of the descent into degradation and the long struggle to pull herself out again.

She is now 56 and the street is seven years behind her. She is determined to study until she achieves the title of, as she puts it, 'Dr Chris.' 'I want to develop to the point of brilliance,' she says with childlike enthusiasm, 'if it's possible . . .'

She works in the kitchens of the Anglican All Saints Convent in Oxford to help pay for her education. She is a diminutive figure but not in the least petite. All those years on the street have taken their toll. Sleeves pushed up, her strong, heavily scarred and tattooed bare arms look menacing. The close-cropped hair, weathered face and beefy hands add to the impression.

But the toughness is not even skin-deep. Someone recently described her as a 'wizened old gnome.' She had to look up 'wizened' in the dictionary, and what she found upset her greatly. It is hard for her to be reminded of her past. The shame is still unbearable.

Born illegitimate in 1938, Kitch grew up in the slums of Bradford, on Tumbling Hill Street. Her mother was a domestic servant and married Kitch's stepfather, a labourer, purely to give her child a name. Kitch's stepfather regularly beat her.

There was one fleeting moment of distinction in her childhood. Kitch, an avid reader with a deep desire to become a scholar – the only route she could see out of the slums – got a scholarship to the local grammar school.

But the class chasm was unbridgeable. Her classmates included the daughters of the lord mayor and the chief constable. 'I was with a group of people who spoke a different language,' she says, 'The whole school was about a different language.' It was a chasm too wide for the girl from Tumbling Hill Street. There were gaffes and embarrassing incidents; she was not surprised when she was asked to leave.

While going through a series of dead-end jobs – clippie, laundry worker, mill labourer – she started hanging out with a crowd in town. After the rejections of the grammar school girls, she had at last found acceptance. Soon she was drinking heavily and taking drugs.

From here, Kitch's story becomes fragmented, the memories no longer sharp: three children, each taken away; shoplifting; prison. On the streets. In hospital. And back on the streets.

She ended up in London, where the area around Piccadilly became her 'patch.' Amid the myriad daily degradations, two incidents stand out in her mind. The first occurred in Soho. Wandering aimlessly in clubland, she noticed a man with no legs propelling himself with his hands on a kind of skateboard. His torso was massive and his face full of cruelty. 'I was trapped,' she says. 'I knew this man was an abuser; and I knew that whatever he said, I would do. It shows just how messed up I was.'

Accompanying the man on the skateboard was another, equally odd dog, making what Kitch describes as 'obscene noises.' She found herself walking with them to a telephone booth. Inside, the legless man ripped off her trousers and raped her. While she says she had become used to rape on the streets, there was something particularly debasing about this incident.

For a while after the violation, she wandered the streets. Kitch believes it is an indication of her madness that she could not think of anything better to do than return to where the rape had occurred. She gazed at the spot, then climbed on to a nearby wall and dived, head first, on to the pavement, smashing her eye. That put her back in hospital.

The second incident was the turning point. Asleep in a doorway, she was awoken by what seemed to be a spray of rain on her face. Opening her eyes, she saw a policeman. It wasn't rain. She was paralysed with shame at the disdain on his face as he zipped up his fly. Kitch neither moved nor spoke as she watched him turn away from where she lay huddled.

'Is this what I have become?' she thought. 'People even piss on me now, and it doesn't matter.' This was her lowest point. She stank. She was filthy. A mad woman staggering around. 'The ridicule was unbearable,' she says.

Although not religious, Chris prayed. She didn't know what else to do. 'I prayed to God, whatever God was. I knew I couldn't take any more. I just said, "What do I do? Please help me".'

The answer to her prayer, she decided, was to stop the drugs. Not easy. But at least she knew what she had to do. She found a rehabilitation centre and was admitted.

There were plenty of false starts. On one occasion, resentful of some of the inmates who kept their distance from her, she got drunk and robbed the place of £200. 'I didn't know how to deal with resentment,' she says. She was 47 by then, and no one thought she would ever get it together.

After so long on the streets, there were many things – particularly to do with emotions – that she didn't understand. She had to be told, for example, to smile at people, something that had never occurred to her before. And every time she failed, she would go back to the old life.

After an arrest for shoplifting, a probation officer shrewdly pointed out: 'The drugs might not kill you, Chris, but the shame – the degradation – will. You are lacerating yourself with behaviour that degrades you in your own eyes.'

That got to her as no words from a professional ever had. With the help of Alcoholics Anonymous and Narcotics Anonymous, she has managed not to drink or take drugs since 1987. With the aid of a counsellor, she learnt that the key to everything is to feel good about yourself; if you do something that is wrong, you make amends. So she took on a cleaning job to pay back the treatment centre she had robbed.

She was ready to continue where she had left off so many years before, to become a scholar. The counsellor guided her on what courses to take, and her academic career began there.

Once she has gained the right qualifications, her plan is to do whatever she can for other women trapped on the street. While her job at the convent, where she also lives

in a residential flat, does not provide enough money for her to begin her postgraduate studies in October, she is determined she will find it somehow. 'I know I have a lot to give, and I want to learn how to give it.'

At an age at which many people are preparing for retirement, she feels her productive life has just begun; she weight-trains, plays table tennis in the Oxford league, has learnt to sleep in a bed...

'Chris has seen another world and clawed her way out in an incredibly courageous and creative way,' says Dr Wendy Wheeler, one

of Kitch's former tutors at North London University.

I ask Chris if she now gives money to people she sees slumped in doorways. 'Sometimes, but not often,' she replies, 'because I don't want to enable them to stay in doorways. Am I really helping them, or am I just helping my guilt? I hurt when I see them but I'm powerless to help them. You give people money in doorways, and they are not going to come out of doorways.'

© The Telegraph Plc
London, 1995

Reasons for homelessness

The reasons for homelessness are many; some people have to leave a home they had:

- My home was attached to my job.
- My partner was violent.
- We got behind with the mortgage when interest rates went up.
- I got ill and couldn't keep up the rent.
- The landlord wanted us out – he had others who would pay more.

Some people have left an institution:

- I've been in care.
- The hospital I was in was closed.
- I've been released from prison.

Others have never had a home of their own:

- I've been staying with friends, but there's just no more room.
- My parents' house is far too overcrowded now.
- I'm looking for work – there's no work to be found where my parents live.
- I'm a refugee.

There are many reasons, some are given in the table below:

	%
Parents/relatives no longer able to accommodate	33
Breakdown/spouse/partner	17
Mortgage/arrears	8
Rent arrears:	
– local authority	1
– private sector	1
Loss of tied/rented accommodation	20
Other	16

NB   These are the reasons for homelessness given by those accepted as homeless (and therefore eligible for help). The figures do not include single people or childless couples, or those who are not accepted as homeless by local councils.

The above is an extract from: *Housing and Homelessness Information Pack* available from CHAS (The Catholic Housing Aid Society). See page 39 for address details.

© CHAS
June, 1994

It could happen to you

On the streets of London

By Aileen Wright

Part and parcel of being homeless is telling your story. Everybody has some kind of fascination with the idea, perhaps because they want reassurance that it would not happen to them. In fact, though, it could, because the streets have no prejudice.

I came to London when I was 18 to escape from small-town England. I had made up my mind to study for my A-levels. The sixth form college I chose was able to send me lists of landlords' names and addresses.

I was lucky enough, to start with. I landed up in a pleasant bedsit near the college. The landlady did not require much of a deposit and was willing to wait patiently for months until my housing benefit came through. Most private landlords in London are much stricter than that.

In the final year of my course, I moved in with two friends who both had fathers who were well off, so our difficulty over the deposit miraculously disappeared. I was so pleased to get a room of my own that I just assumed that the six-month lease would be renewed when the time came round. The flat was wonderful – we had our own kitchen – and a back yard for my cat to patrol.

The tenancy of the flat ran out in the month of my exams. The flat was in a bad state of repair, but the landlord simply wanted to patch things up so that they looked presentable. He refused to give back our deposit money, and my friends' fathers had decided not to be so generous this time.

So there I was, facing the most difficult exams of my life with a hungry cat and a few boxes of possessions. I knew a number of squats in the area, and moved in with a friend. How I managed to sit my exams in the knowledge that I could be out on the streets that night, I will never know.

I then began to move from shelter to shelter, taking whatever was available: friends' floors, squats, empty buildings. I spent most of my days begging for money for food. I learned very quickly whom to trust and whom not to trust and became very suspicious towards any form of authority: particularly the Department of Social Security and the police, who were the main obstacles to my surviving in that way. But I always had someone with whom to share the time of day and have a laugh.

> **I was lucky enough, to start with. I landed up in a pleasant bedsit near the college.**

After about six months of this existence the council housed me and my boyfriend in a bed and breakfast place. But my ever-patient cat, who had stayed with me in all sorts of conditions was not allowed in. I was always told that cats cannot stand instability and change, preferring a secure home to a different, strange

> **I suppose all I needed was for some one to give me a chance, and that is what people who are down on their luck so often never get**

place each night. But this cat never ran away. I found her a home, but parting was really hard. My cat was the only thing I put before myself.

Things went well enough at first. But I was once more reliant on my fortnightly pittance from the state. For two weeks I would be broke, living off Kwik-Save baked beans and cigarette butt roll-ups. By the time your allowance turns up, you just want to enjoy yourself for as long as you can.

The owner of the hostel had been trying to sell it for quite some time. But no one wanted to buy a run-down social security building, especially in the middle of a long-term recession. So after a while he just forgot about the place. The first thing to go was the breakfasts (paid for in the housing benefit we received), soon followed by the staff and the payphone. Then one day I returned to find the building plunged into darkness, and the residents gathered round candles in the kitchen, which was filthy by now. There was a mother with a one-year-old child among the residents and children need electricity even more than adults to cater for their needs.

In my begging days, I was befriended by one of the vendors of the *Big Issue* – the paper which helps the homeless to help themselves because they buy it for 25p and are authorised to sell it for 60p. He was constantly on at me to do the same. It took me ages to get round to it, for the first step out of a rut is the most difficult. As a vendor, I was able to make some money legally. From then on, things moved so quickly I hardly had time to glance back.

I suppose all I needed was for some one to give me a chance, and that is what people who are down on their luck so often never get.

© *The Tablet*
December, 1994

Refugees and asylum seekers

From the British Red Cross

Who is a refugee?

According to the UN Convention Relating to the Status of Refugees (1951) and its Protocol (1967), a refugee is someone who has left their country 'owing to a well-founded fear of being persecuted for reasons of race, religion, nationality, membership of a particular social group or political opinion'.

The official use of the term 'refugee' reflects the above definition. However, it is more often used to mean all people who have fled their homes because of fear for their own safety. Technically, a refugee must have crossed an international border. People who have not done so are known as 'internally displaced' or 'displaced persons.' A person is not officially recognised as a 'refugee' until the authorities of the country to which they have fled, or other international body, have investigated their circumstances and reasons for flight and decided that they can be recognised as a refugee according to the Convention. Until that decision has been made, they are known as an 'asylum seeker.'

Anyone can become a refugee. The decision to leave home is usually the last resort – 'a refugee is a person who does not want to be a refugee' (Perico Rodriguez – a refugee in the UK). Many people have been forced to leave their homes because of their religion, their social or ethnic background, or for their political opinions. There are many other reasons why people leave their homes, including war, armed conflict, persecution, human rights violations, poverty and famine. Some of these reasons are not reflected in the UN Convention or Protocol. Broader definitions of who is a refugee are, however, incorporated in other international regional instruments, such as the Organisation of African Unity's (OAU) Convention Governing the Specific Aspects of Refugee Problems in Africa (1969) and in the Cartagena Declaration (1984), signed by 10 Latin American countries. Other international legal instruments relating to refugees, include the 1948 Universal Declaration of Human Rights, which declares that 'Everyone has the right to seek and enjoy in other countries asylum from persecution'.

The UN estimates that there are 23 million refugees in the world today, as well as some 25 – 30 million displaced people.

Refugees in the UK

It is very difficult to get an accurate picture of refugees in the UK. Various organisations and authorities have tried to work out the numbers currently in the UK. A survey conducted by the World University Service UK in 1993 (in WUS *Refugee Education Handbook*, 1994) estimated that there are around 250,000 refugees in the UK, of whom 200,000 are in the Greater London area. The greatest concentrations of refugees outside London are in the West Midlands, Scotland, Wales and the North East, with the largest groups originating from Iran, Turkey, Somalia, Uganda, Sri Lanka, former Yugoslavia, Vietnam, Eritrea, Ethiopia and Iraq.

Home Office statistics for 1994 indicate that 32,830 applications were made for asylum in the UK. In the same year, 825 asylum seekers were recognised as refugees under the 1951 UN Convention, with a further 3,660 applicants refused asylum but granted Exceptional Leave to Remain (ELR) in the UK. A total of 357 unaccompanied children, aged 17 or under, applied for asylum at ports of entry in 1994.

How does the British Red Cross help refugees and asylum seekers?

As a member of the International Red Cross Movement, the British Red Cross works in partnership with the International Committee of the Red Cross (CRC), the International Federation of Red Cross and Red Crescent Societies, and many National Societies. They are all involved in various activities relating to refugees, in the countries from which refugees are fleeing as well as in those to which they flee, in addition to those in situations of internal displacement. Such assistance involves medical and food relief, hygiene supplies, medical assistance, visiting prisoners of war (POWs) and detainees, and facilitating family communications.

The International Movement of Red Cross and Red Crescent Societies has pledged itself to 'at all times be ready to assist and to protect refugees, displaced persons and returnees' (1981 Manila Statement) and has issued various Resolutions on assistance to these groups. This continues its long history of assisting refugees. During the First World War, for example, the Red Cross ran relief operations to assist displaced persons and POWs in Russia. The Red Cross sent food parcels and family messages to POWs and detainees in concentration camps. At the end of this war, with 30-40 million displaced people throughout Europe, the ICRC issued travel documents enabling people to travel home or to a country of asylum. The ICRC's Central Tracing Agency (CTA) enabled millions of people to learn of the whereabouts of captured, missing and released people. The ICRC also has a special responsibility to assist internally displaced people.

The British Red Cross is committed to the humanitarian aims of the International Movement, upon which it bases all its actions and activities. The Movement respects the seven Fundamental Principles of Humanity, Impartiality, Neutrality, Independence, Voluntary Service, Unity and Universality; people are helped according to their needs, irrespective of their status, nationality, etc., with the focus being

upon bringing assistance to the most vulnerable people throughout the world. It is not a campaigning or pressure organisation.

The British Red Cross has been involved in providing medical assistance to refugees in Hong Kong and tracing the families of unaccompanied children in Rwanda and neighbouring countries, in addition to supplying food, water facilities and shelter to refugees in many other parts of the world.

Core Services in the UK

The British Red Cross offers a range of 'core' services, including Medical Loan, Transport & Escort, International Tracing and Red Cross Messages, First Aid training and provision, Nursing Support and Youth Activities. Refugees and asylum seekers, as all vulnerable groups and others requiring BRCS assistance, can avail themselves of these services.

International Tracing Services

BRCS has been helping refugees and asylum seekers in the UK to keep in touch with their family members overseas for many years, through the International Tracing and Message Services.

Armed conflict and political upheaval often tear families apart: some people are forced to leave the country, fearing for their safety. They may leave loved ones behind, or be separated from them whilst they flee to different countries. Not having news of, and not knowing the fate of one's relatives is very traumatic. The Red Cross can help people to trace their family members and to keep in touch with them. All enquiries are treated in the strictest confidence; after many years and changes in circumstances, traced relatives may not wish to have contact with or to give any information to their families. The Red Cross respects these wishes.

Red Cross messages

Red Cross Messages can be used when telephone, postal and other normal communications break down, such as in Somalia or in Bosnia. The relative in the UK can contact the British Red Cross to write a Red Cross Message (RCM) to their family overseas. RCMs are open messages containing news of a family or personal nature. No military, political or otherwise controversial information can be included. Each message contains a space for the addressee to reply to the sender. RCMs are used today in many countries where there is conflict, including Sri Lanka, Somalia, Bosnia, Angola, Rwanda, Afghanistan, the Yemen and the Sudan.

© *British Red Cross*

A great tragedy of our time

From the United Nations High Commissioner for Refugees

As long as there have been wars, persecution, discrimination and intolerance, there have been refugees.

They are of every race and religion and can be found in every part of the world.

Forced to flee out of fear for their lives and liberty, refugees often give up everything – home, belongings, family and country – for an uncertain future in a strange land.

Their plight is one of the great tragedies of our time and their fate is linked to political and human rights questions that should be of concern to each and every one of us.

Helping the world's 20.7 million refugees is the job of the United Nations High Commissioner for Refugees, which was created by the UN General Assembly and began work in 1951.

UNHCR's founding mandate defines refugees as those who have fled their countries because of a well-founded fear of persecution for reasons of their race, religion, nationality, political opinion or membership of a particular social group and who cannot or do not want to return.

Since its creation, UNHCR has helped tens of millions of refugees, earning two Nobel Peace Prizes in the process.

But the refugee problem continues to grow, more than doubling over the past decade. Each day in 1992, an average of 10,000 people fled their homes because of war, human rights abuses and persecution.

Today, there are 20.7 million refugees around the world and another 25 million men, women and children are displaced in their own lands. One in every 122 people on earth has been forced into flight.

And refugees do not just come from the Third World. In the heart of Europe, more than 4 million people have been driven from their homes in the continent's biggest refugee crisis since World War II.

Photo: UNHCR / L Taylor

Many Mozambican children were born abroad and will see their country for the first time.

Fortunately, many refugees spend only a short time away from their homes. But millions of others languish for years in dismal, isolated camps before solutions can be found.

Despite the efforts of more than 3,000 UNHCR workers in 193 offices in 114 countries, the refugee problem remains a worldwide tragedy.

Would you slam the door on Einstein?

Refugees are not faceless people begging for our sympathy. They are people just like us who through no fault of their own were caught up in some of the greatest upheavals of the 20th century.

They are doctors and lawyers, teachers and truck drivers, farmers and fishermen, mothers and fathers and children.

And they are people who, given a chance, can contribute to the good of us all.

Albert Einstein and Sigmund Freud were refugees. So were Spanish President Felipe Gonzalez Marquez, Portuguese President Mario Soares, and former Philippine President Corazon Aquino.

Other famous refugees include Mikhail Baryshnikov, Rudolf Nureyev, Marlene Dietrich, Aleksandr Solzhenitsyn, Bertolt Brecht, Sun Yat-sen, Richard Wagner, Victor Hugo, Giuseppe Garibaldi, Vladimir Nabokov and Marc Chagall. What if the world had turned its back on these people?

Where are all the refugees?

Refugees are all over the world but most have found sanctuary in developing countries.

Southwest Asia, North Africa and the Middle East	5,493,000
Africa	5,889,000
Europe	7,493,000
The Americas	838,000
Asia and Oceania	1,024,000

In their own words

The refugee's story is never a happy one. But amid the pain and deprivation emerge many examples of perseverance and courage. Here are a few of them.

'In my home town there was fighting everywhere. There were so many people fleeing down the road with nothing. No clothes, no food. We came to a place where there were mines. Someone was blown up and everyone started running and there was blood everywhere. We saw villages where there was nobody, not even a cat. People started eating leaves. People began to die. One old man sat in the road and said he couldn't walk any more. He died an hour later. When we got to the river, planes dropped bombs on us but we finally made it across the border and to this camp. Now UNHCR gives us food and we even have a school.'

A Sudanese refugee child in Kenya

'I'm still in contact with my mother, though I'll probably never see her again. She is the only person I've told where I am. I wish she could meet my fiancee, but it won't be before my country is free again.'

A man who found sanctuary in the United States

'My husband was a musician. He made records and was well known. Suddenly, the government didn't like his music any more and he was banned from the radio and his songs were prohibited. But my husband had always sung what he wanted. Music cannot conform, he told them, so they threatened him with prison. We fled. What can we do? These aren't happy times.'

A woman refugee in Europe

UNHCR

The right to seek asylum

The Universal Declaration of Human Rights states that everyone has the right to seek and enjoy asylum from persecution.

But protecting that right isn't easy. Countries of first asylum, often poor themselves, sometimes grow weary of the needs of those being given sanctuary. Occasionally, they try to push refugees back across the border.

And people in rich countries, fearing that the influx of asylum seekers is becoming unmanageable, sometimes slam doors in their faces. UNHCR strives to re-open doors and keep them open.

UNHCR's most important function is known as 'international protection'. This means that UNHCR strives to ensure that no refugee is returned involuntarily to a country where he or she has reason to fear persecution.

UNHCR also promotes adherence to international agreements on refugees and monitors the behavior of individual states to ensure that they respect those agreements. When refugees are mistreated or forcibly repatriated, UNHCR protests to governments at the highest level.

UNHCR's challenge

UNHCR helps those forced into flight to save their lives or liberty. Sometimes these include mass movements of people fleeing civil conflict and other man-made disasters. Over the years, UNHCR also has been asked by the UN Secretary-General to assist people internally displaced in their own lands.

First, refugees must be protected, against physical harm and being forcibly returned to countries where they would be in danger.

UNHCR also provides assistance like food, water, shelter and medical care.

And, always, UNHCR seeks durable, long-term solutions for the plight of refugees – voluntary repatriation back to their original homes, integration in the countries where they first sought asylum, or resettlement to a third country.

Voluntary repatriation is the best solution because the right to return to one's homeland is as sacred as the right to seek asylum. But return is not always possible because it usually requires elimination of the conditions which sent the refugees into exile in the first place.

So, UNHCR helps some refugees build new lives in the countries where they first sought asylum. When necessary, UNHCR assists refugees to resettle in third countries.

Refugees dream of home

Because of the huge sacrifices involved, most people become refugees only after a long and agonizing appraisal.

So the first step toward helping refugees is to understand that they are not a threat to you. Rather, they are themselves threatened.

Indeed, most refugees dream of the day they can return home in dignity and safety to resume life in their own land.

As an apolitical and humanitarian organization, it is UNHCR's job to see that this dream comes true for as many refugees as possible.

Backed by voluntary contributions from governments, other organizations and individuals, UNHCR has already helped millions of refugees pick up the pieces of their lives.

But millions of others still need your help and understanding. We need your help to help refugees.

UNCHR Action
P.O Box 2500
CH – 1211
Geneva 2
Switzerland
© UNHCR

Children: a right to refuge

From Save the Children

A refugee

In international law, a refugee is someone who has fled from his or her home country or is unable to return to it 'owing to a well-founded fear of being persecuted for reasons of race, religion, nationality, membership of a particular social group or political opinion' (1951 UN Convention Relating to the Status of Refugees). This definition was designed to apply to refugees in Europe in the aftermath of the Second World War. A 1967 Protocol extended it to refugees in other parts of the world.

A displaced person

A displaced person is someone who has been forced to moved to another part of their country because of war, famine or disaster. Unlike refugees who have crossed an international border, displaced people are not legally entitled to international protection. The official figure for the world's refugees now stands at a record 18.9 million. More than half of them are children.

An explosion of ethnic and civil conflicts, including those in the former Eastern Bloc, means that actual numbers are much larger. People made homeless within their own countries are not included in the official refugee figures: estimates suggest that there may be as many as 30 million. On average, 2,700 people flee their homes every day to escape famine and conflict.

More than four decades after the 1951 Convention Relating to the Status of Refugees, the system put in place to protect refugees is under severe strain. For the fist time since the Second World War, military assistance has been required to protect agencies delivering aid to thousands in Eastern Europe and the Horn of Africa.

Save the Children

Global political and economic upheavals signal more refugee crises ahead, increasing pressure on the international community and its ability to cope. As the numbers of refugees and displaced people grow, millions of others are returning home to disaster areas devastated by years of war.

Close links between political action and humanitarian action in the current crises in Somalia and former Yugoslavia have enabled more flexible and effective delivery of aid to those people in need, but major changes are still needed in the long term. As new emergencies arise, the pie of humanitarian aid is cut into ever smaller slices.

Key issues

The plight of refugee and displaced adults and children is one of the great humanitarian crises of our time. Based on its experience of working with refugee and displaced children, Save the Children is continuing to push for change at the highest level. Its main concerns are:

- Governments should ensure that refugees and displaced people have access to food in line with their basic human rights.

- Special attention should be paid to the needs and rights of refugee and displaced children, especially those without families, in accordance with the UN Convention on the Rights of the Child and UNHCR's Guidelines on Refugee Children.

- The wider needs of refugees including clean water, shelter, medical provision and education should not be neglected. Their right to trade and work and their freedom of movement should be guaranteed.

- The roles and responsibilities of the relevant UN agencies concerned with refugees and displaced people should be clarified and, if necessary, their mandates extended to reflect contemporary realities. The 'cross-mandate' approach requires adequate planning and resourcing.

- International law and international mechanisms for the assistance and protection of displaced people must be strengthened. They should become the responsibility of a specific UN agency.

- Donor governments must ensure that UNHCR is adequately funded so that it can fulfil its functions on a regular and reliable basis.

- The international community must support the implementation of the 1992 UN Resolution (46/182) on the strengthening of the co-ordination of humanitarian assistance by the UN, and the new Department of Humanitarian Affairs must be properly resourced to ensure an effective system for aid delivery.

The International System and the Role of UNHCR

International laws to protect refugees do exist, based on rights defined in the United Nations Charter, the Universal Declaration of Human Rights, and statements of rights and obligations under international law. National governments, as members of the UN and signatories to the 1951 Refugee Convention, are obliged to protect refugees politically and physically. It is the role of the Office of the High Commissioner for Refugees (UNHCR), the UN agency set up in 1950, to:

- promote international standards for the treatment of refugees.
- make sure that these are enforced in such areas as employment, education, residence and freedom of movement.
- safeguard against refugees being returned to a country where they may face persecution.

Immediate relief

Where no rapid solution can be found, UNHCR provides or co-ordinates immediate relief, including supplies of food, shelter, water, health services, sanitation, clothing and education. A new emergency fund of $50m has been authorised for a new unit set up in 1992: the Department of Humanitarian Affairs. This houses the Emergency Preparedness and Response Section, with staff and resources on permanent standby. Five new emergency officers with regional responsibilities are deployed in the field to lead rapid response teams made up of specialists in emergency relief.

UNHCR's relief programmes are run together with host governments, other UN agencies (particularly the World Food) Programme (WFP) which provides the majority of food aid) and non-governmental organisations such as Save the Children.

UNHCR depends on voluntary annual subscriptions from national governments. Its income in 1992 was $1 billion, a shortfall of $100 million on its stated global requirements.

New responses to co-ordinated emergency action include the 'cross-mandate' approach being used in Ethiopia. Traditional assistance based on individual registration and entitlement can be problematic in areas where instability and poverty conspire to make the host community equally needy. Under the cross-mandate approach, the needs of the entire community are assessed, including the needs of 'official' refugees, internally displaced people, drought victims, demobilised soldiers and returnees.

Lasting solutions

UNHCR's main role has always been to seek lasting solutions to the problems of refugees. These include voluntary repatriation or resettlement.

In practice, UNHCR has worked to meet the needs of a broader category of people than those officially defined as refugees. These are mostly people who have been uprooted by war. UNHCR is also increasingly involved with 'returnees' such as those returning to Afghanistan from Pakistan and from Malawi to Mozambique.

But the result of extending the authority of UNHCR to caring for displaced people and returnees has spread its limited resources more thinly. This lack of resources seriously undermines UNHCR's ability to fulfil its role in 'searching for lasting solutions', including voluntary repatriation, the best permanent solution.

REFUGEES BY CONTINENT

Region	Dec 1992
Africa	5,130,000
The Americas	1,927,000
Asia & Oceania	1,093,000
Europe	4,407,00
South West Asia and Middle East	6,441,000
Total	**18,998,000**

source: UNHCR

Notes
1. These are provided mostly by governments based on their own records and methods of estimation. In certain instances they include persons reported by Governments to be in 'refugee-like situations'.
2. These do not cover over one million Palestinian refugees. They are registered with the UN Relief and Works Agency (UNRWA)

The role of the international community

The number of refugees has nearly doubled over the last decade: 10 million in 1982 and 18.9 million in 1993.

Donor governments have a clear responsibility to support UNHCR. The responsibilities of countries where refugees seek asylum are also clearly spelt out. If refugees are to be integrated and their dignity respected, they must be granted social and economic rights. It is often overlooked that the rights of refugees do not end once they are granted refugee status and asylum.

Are these rights backed up by law? Yes – both the 1951 Convention and the 1967 Protocol provide for a range of social and economic rights for refugees including public education, employment, self-employment, artistic and legal status, welfare and social security. Many states grant those rights in a limited way.

But refugees and displaced people increasingly seek refuge in countries where the host government's services to its own civilians – for example health care and education – fall far below acceptable minimum levels. Many such countries in Africa have chronic food crises and economies on the edge of collapse. Yet these countries are expected to provide for massive and unpredictable influxes of people.

- Yemen, one of the poorest countries on earth, is now sheltering some 56,204 Somali refugees.
- Kenya's total refugee population is 400,000, the fastest growing number of refugees in the world outside former Yugoslavia.
- There are approximately 3.93 million displaced people in former Yugoslavia.
- In many recent instances, the international community has failed in its responsibility to respond quickly and effectively to dramatic and unexpected mass movements of people.
- In June 1992, some 1,500 Bhutanese refugees died in camps in Nepal before international assistance was mobilised.

© Save the Children November, 1994

Refugee children fleeing war 'need better support'

Glenda Cooper

Thousands of refugee children who escape to Britain from the trauma of war may be going without vital support, according to the mental health charity, Young Minds.

Launching its fourth report in the Violence and Young Minds campaign today, the charity demands a network of properly resourced child and family mental health services throughout Britain, with adequate central funding to provide English as a second language in schools.

The report, *War and Refugee Children*, says 23,500 such children are currently living in Britain, with 85 per cent of those in London. Between 250 and 500 enter Britain unaccompanied each year, of whom half will end up in children's homes.

Refugees' problems are exacerbated by the fact that most do not receive full refugee status. In the second half of last year, 77 per cent of applications for political asylum were rejected. Of the rest, only 5 per cent were granted full refugee status, with the other 18 per cent given 'exceptional leave to remain', which does not bring the same entitlement to benefit, education and housing.

Before July last year, anyone applying for asylum had the same rights to permanent local authority accommodation as anyone who was homeless and categorised as being in priority need. Since then, local authorities have had the option to give asylum-seekers temporary accommodation.

'At the moment there are absolutely no services whatsoever,' Jill Rutter, education officer of the Refugee Council, said; 'They are left to their own devices. Young people of 14 to 15 are particularly vulnerable.'

Steve Flood, author of the report, said mental health problems associated with exposure to armed conflict should be taken more seriously. 'Children become very withdrawn, become aggressive, suffer eating disorders, sleeping problems. Somatic problems are very common – headaches, stomach aches, physical pain – but the most worrying aspects are associated with bad concentration and impaired memory, which holds back their development at school and in society.'

> **Between 250 and 500 refugee children enter Britain unaccompanied each year, of whom half will end up in children's homes**

Throughout the century the proportion of civilians among the casualties of war has increased enormously. While only one in ten casualties were civilians in the First World War, by the Second World War, 50 per cent of casualties were civilian, and over the past 10 years this proportion has risen to 75 per cent. According to UNICEF, between 1980 and 1990, 1.5 million children died in war, 4 million were left injured and 10 million were traumatised.

The research assimilated by the charity suggests that children cope better in a stable environment such as a school. The charity is therefore calling for schools to provide training for teachers on refugee issues and local educational authorities to provide a special co-ordinator.

Young Minds is also campaigning to secure funding for English as a second language, which was previously given out under Section 11 of the 1966 Local Government Act. From April next year more than half this money will be put into the Single Regeneration Budget, which means language funding will be competing with urban regeneration projects.

© *The Independent*
October, 1994

Refugees and displaced people

Information from Oxfam

Most of Oxfam's work with refugees and displaced people begins with an urgent need to respond quickly, providing emergency relief in the form of water supplies, shelter, food, basic medical supplies, and clothing. Between April 1993 and February 1994, Oxfam spent £23,608,724 on emergency work, mostly in situations involving refugees and displaced people.

Oxfam also provides long-term help for those who are working to build new lives, either in new surroundings, or back home if they are able to return.

There are far more women than men in most refugee populations. This makes it essential that their particular needs are considered when planning and carrying out relief, and longer-term programmes of work.

Afghanistan

In the area of Pul-i-Khumri, Oxfam is working with people who have fled from conflict in the capital, Kabul. Oxfam co-ordinates much of its work in camps through women's committees, experience having shown this to be the most effective way of reaching the greatest number of families. Oxfam has helped to build several communal 'tandoor' ovens, enabling the families to make their traditional bread. The area around each oven serves as an informal meeting place for the women, where they discuss their problems and possible solutions. Representatives from each block of tents then talk to project workers, enabling Oxfam's work plans to be well informed by the women themselves.

Oxfam provides a sanitation and water-supply programme in the camps, as well as shelter materials, and advice on basic health care. Sorya, is 30 years old and has been in Shamarq Camp for one year. She, her husband, and their six children fled from Kabul by bus, to get away from the fighting. She told Oxfam workers; 'It is very cold [in the tents], but it is better to be here than in Kabul, because at least here it is peaceful.'

Economic migration

Many poor countries do not have the means to provide for their citizens. Repayment of debts owed to The World Bank, IMF, and governments and banks in the North often makes it impossible for governments in the South to invest in the public services or economic development that would create jobs for their citizens. Many people decide to escape poverty and lack of opportunity in their own country and move away to earn a living. Many will leave their families in order to find work, and send money home.

There are thought to be 20 – 40 million undocumented economic migrants in the world today.* Around 80 per cent of the foreign-currency earnings in countries like Egypt and Pakistan comes from money sent home by migrant workers.

Returning home

When circumstances allow refugees to return home, they often return to face further problems. They may be returning to an area devastated by war; uncleared landmines may pose a threat – restricting movement and greatly hampering people's efforts to rebuild their lives. Homes, other buildings, and equipment may have been destroyed or taken over by other people. Those who stayed behind may resent returnees, because of the added pressure they can place on already meagre resources. For these reasons, it is important for Oxfam to consider the needs of the whole community, and to plan for long-term development.

In Sri Lanka, years of civil war have torn communities apart, damaged the economy and left more than half a million homeless. Oxfam helped large numbers of displaced people living in camps to meet their basic needs.

In eastern Sri Lanka, some families have left the camps and returned to their homes and villages. Thousands have also returned from India under a UNHCR repatriation scheme. Oxfam has worked closely with the Ministry of Resettlement to ensure that resettlement is well planned and co-ordinated.

In the north, Oxfam is helping to renovate irrigation-water tanks that had fallen into disrepair as a result of conflict. Working with local organisations, this kind of project provides work for landless labourers and for the displaced who have settled in the area.

Oxfam is keen to help people to pick up the threads of their lives, and build their confidence in their ability to support themselves.

As the numbers of refugees and displaced people increase, and the situations producing them become more complex, there is an urgent need for the causes of displacement to be addressed. Those without basic rights are the most vulnerable when circumstances around them change. The poor and powerless are the first to suffer in situations that cause displacement.

Oxfam believes all women, men and children should have basic political, economic and social rights: rights not only to food, water and shelter, but also the fundamental human and political rights which are necessary if people are to earn a living in a sustainable way. Sustainable livelihoods are ways in which women and men, on a long-term basis, can earn a living without harming others or the planet.

State of the World's Refugees UNHCR, Penguin Books, 1993

© Oxfam
February, 1995

Buddy system aids school to ease pain of pupils in exile

More than one-third of pupils at the George Orwell School, north London, are refugees. Most turn up in the middle of term, unable to speak English. Many have faced war and death at an early age, their parents have been killed and their lives turned upside down, writes Glenda Cooper

To cope with this, the school, which has 550 pupils aged 11 to 16, has an induction policy. New students are given a yellow card with information about themselves, their class and their timetable. There is someone to help those who do not speak English and lose their way, and each child is given a 'buddy' – a child speaking their language charged with looking after them.

'I think the first day was the worst,' Cecilia, from Bolivia, said; 'I was scared I wouldn't find my way around school. It was hard because I couldn't speak English and I didn't know what everyone was talking about. I thought they must all be talking about me.'

Chaltu, whose family was killed in the civil war in Ethiopia, said: 'Every night I would go home and pray to God I would learn more English. I couldn't speak to anyone and I couldn't understand. But we started ESL (English as a second language) in our first week and had two lessons a week.'

'You miss your friends in your country,' she added; 'It's very hard not to go back and see your home. They killed my dad and my brother. My uncle is dead, my cousin is dead. They would catch us if we went back because our family was in the newspapers.'

'We try to do most of our work alongside other pupils,' David Davies, head of the three ESL teachers in the school, said; 'We wanted to keep them in mainstream teaching, and work with the other teachers adapting subjects so bilingual students can understand.

'But it's very, very difficult only having three ESL teachers. Often you feel like you've got your back against the wall. There is not enough staff to cope with the kids' needs.'

The refugees here are highly motivated students: 'They are strong kids,' Caroline Lodge, the head-teacher, said; 'They are not here to freeload but to make the most of themselves and then go back and help their country.'

Gulistan, a Kurd from Turkey, and Chaltu want to be lawyers. 'We know how it feels to suffer,' Chaltu said, 'and that is why we want to help other people.'

Most want to return. 'It is so different to here. Here there is peace everywhere and no political problems. My heart is in my country,' Gulistan said.

Ms Lodge sees the school as essential to the healing process. 'We need to have caring adults providing a good strong environment for them to work through their feelings. The school can be reassuring for these children who have had so much instability in their life, just to know the same teacher will be in the same place every day.'

© The Independent
October, 1994

Photo: UNHCR / B Press

We know how it feels to suffer.

Promoting solutions

From The United Nations High Commissioner for Refugees (UNCHR)

In seeking durable solutions to refugees' problems, UNHCR attempts to help those who wish to go home. Where repatriation is not feasible, it helps to integrate refugees in countries of asylum or, failing that, to resettle them in other countries.

Voluntary Repatriation

Voluntary repatriation has long been regarded as the preferred solution to refugee problems. In 1993 over 1.8 million persons returned to their countries of origin, notably Afghanistan, Cambodia, Ethiopia, Myanmar and Somalia. Return movements have continued in 1994. UNHCR's approach to voluntary repatriation depends on a number of factors, most importantly conditions in the country of origin. Unless it is convinced that refugee can return in reasonable safety, the organisation does not actively promote return. It may, however, facilitate existing spontaneous movements – as, for example, through the travel and in-kind grants it has provided to Afghans returning from Pakistan and the Islamic Republic of Iran. In some cases, where conditions in the country of origin permit, it may actively promote and organise the return movement – as was the case with the 41,000 refugees airlifted home to Namibia in 1989 or the 387,000 Cambodian refugees who went home from Thailand in 1992 and early 1993. In other instances, it promotes repatriation and provides assistance to returnees, but only organises transport for people unable to make their own arrangement. Such has been the approach to the repatriation of some 1.7 million Mozambican refugees that got under way in mid-1993, paving the way for a resolution of the largest single refugee problem on the African continent.

Photo: UNHCR / A Höllmann

Children make the best of any situation: here playing 'truck driver'

Where voluntary repatriation is organized or facilitated by UNHCR, the Office attempts, wherever possible, to ensure that a legal framework is set up to protect the returnees' rights and interests. Steps taken include negotiating amnesties and guarantees of non-recrimination against returnees. Wherever possible, these form the substance of written repatriation agreements. Frequently, tripartite agreements are drawn up between the country of origin, the country of asylum and UNHCR, specifying the conditions of return and setting out safeguards for returnees.

Nevertheless, optimism about voluntary repatriation has been tempered by the fact that many refugees return to situations of devastation and uncertainty or even outright insecurity. UNHCR is therefore adopting new approaches in order to ensure the sustainability of its repatriation and reintegration efforts. In south-eastern Ethiopia, where the situation is one of general deprivation, it has ceased to distinguish between refugees, returnees and affected local people. In a co-operative effort with other United Nations and non-governmental agencies, the organisation has moved beyond its traditional mandate in an attempt to meet the needs of the entire community, stabilise the population and pre-empt renewed displacement.

In other repatriation operations, from Central America to Cambodia and Somalia, UNHCR has increasingly opted for 'quick impact projects' (QIPs) – often in collaboration with UNDP – to help returnees and their communities regain self-sufficiency. Such projects may include the repair and reconstruction of essential facilities such as schools, health centres, roads and bridges, the boosting of the agricultural sector through the provision of livestock, seeds, processing machinery and transport, or the establishment of small scale businesses in rural and urban areas. By filling the gap which has traditionally existed between returnee relief operations and longer-term development efforts, QIPs have become known as a 'bridge to development'.

Local settlement

In cases where voluntary repatriation is unlikely to take place in the foreseeable future, the best solution is often to settle refugees in their host country. This can only be done, however, with the agreement of the Government of the asylum country concerned and, as refugee numbers have escalated, local settlement opportunities have tended to become increasingly restricted.

In industrialized countries, government welfare systems and NGOs provide the bulk of the resources necessary to integrate refugees. Elsewhere, UNHCR furnishes varying degrees of support for local settlement projects in both rural and urban settings. Traditionally, local integration projects in rural areas have taken the form of settlements. In urban or semi-urban areas, assistance is given to individual refugees to help them integrate. When possible, UNHCR provides education, vocational training and counselling to help refugees gain access to employment and the means to become independent.

Third country resettlement

For refugees who can neither return to their country of origin nor safely remain in their country of refuge, the only solution is to resettle in a third country. A number of countries offer asylum to refugees only on a temporary basis on condition that they are subsequently resettled. Even in countries that do not impose this condition, local economic, political or security factors may sometimes make it necessary to move the refugee elsewhere

The decision to resettle a refugee is normally taken only in the absence of other options and when there is no alternative way to guarantee the legal or physical security of the person concerned. In 1993 UNHCR sought resettlement opportunities for some 75,000 persons, the largest group being refugees from the Middle East.

© UNHCR
February, 1995

On the move

Currently, there are over 23 million refugees and others of concern to UNHCR and an additional 26 million internally displaced people (IDPs) in the world. One of every 115 people on earth has been forced into flight.

Global refugee statistics	
Africa	7,450,100
Asia	5,773,500
Europe	6,056,600
Latin America	130,900
North America	1,290,800
Oceania	50,400
Former Soviet Union	2,280,700
Total	**23,033,000**

Note: includes 6,631,100 IDPs and others of concern to UNHCR

Top ten countries of asylum		
Country of asylum	*Country of origin*	*No. of refugees*
Iran (Islamic Rep. of)	Afghanistan/Iraq	2,817,000 *
Zaire	Burundi/Rwanda/Sudan/Angola	1,800,000 *
Pakistan	Afghanistan	1,200,000 *
United States	Various	951,500
Sudan	Chad/Eritrea/Ethiopia/Uganda/Zaire	745,200
Tanzania	Burundi/Rwanda	628,000 *
Guinea	Liberia/Sierra Leone	577,200
Yugoslavia (Fed. Rep. of)	Bosnia/Croatia	499,000 *
Armenia	Azerbaijan/Georgia	340,700
Canada	Various	339,300

Top ten countries of origin		
Country of origin	*Main countries of asylum*	*No. of refugees*
Afghanistan	India/Iran/Pakistan/ Russian Federation	2,950,000 †
Rwanda	Burundi/Tanzania/Uganda/Zaire	2,125,000 †
Liberia	Cote d'Ivoire/Ghana/ Guinea/Sierra Leone	848,000 †
Somalia	Djibouti/Ethiopia/Kenya/Yemen	516,800
Eritrea	Sudan	425,400
Sudan	Ethiopia/Kenya/Uganda/Zaire	391,200
Azerbaijan	Armenia	334,900
Angola	Congo/Zaire/Zambia	325,500
Sierra Leone	Guinea/Liberia	311,100
Burundi	Rwanda/Zaire/Tanzania	271,000 †

† Includes a total of 319,000 IDPs and others of concern in various other countries

Note: All figures date from 31 December 1993 unless indicated

*As of 31 December 1994

© UNHCR

Relief and refuge

The need for emergency aid has never been greater than in the past year. In 1993/94 the ODA (Overseas Development Administration) spent around £179 million on providing timely and effective help for the victims of natural and man-made disasters

The number of people fleeing conflict in parts of Africa, Asia and the former Yugoslavia has risen dramatically. Drought and famine and other natural disasters around the world have added to the problem.

Over the year the ODA provided help for the victims of 135 emergencies. The ODA works as part of the international relief effort and makes sure its activities complement the work of the UN and other relief agencies and donors. All emergency aid is supplied on the basis of identified needs. Frequently, the ODA acts in partnership with non-governmental organisations like the British Red Cross and Oxfam. This relationship is vital. NGOs are often working in the field and have invaluable knowledge of the local situation.

Horn of Africa

Many countries in the Horn of Africa faced another extremely difficult year in 1993. Continuing hostilities in Sudan and drought and pests throughout the area led to poor harvests and shortages of food. When food is in short supply in one area, people start to migrate to another.

This migration creates huge numbers of displaced families in each of the countries and swells the ranks of existing refugees. In Eritrea a bad situation, when the rains failed in July and most of the harvest was lost, was made worse later in the year when swarms of locusts finished off what was left.

Throughout the problems in the Horn, the ODA provided a continuous flow of emergency aid. In January and March, Britain also responded to a number of UN appeals, bringing the British contribution to food needs in the Horn since January 1993 to 155,000 tonnes. The ODA also gave £1 million in August 1993 to the UN Food and Agricultural Organization to combat the plagues of desert locusts threatening food crops throughout the area and elsewhere. In all, the ODA administered nearly £42 million of aid to this part of Africa during the year.

Other emergency aid activities in brief

June 1993: as the peace process in Mozambique gathered momentum after 15 years of civil war, the ODA provided £4 million for 23,000 tonnes of food aid and a further £3 million, channelled through British voluntary organisations, in the form of seeds and tools and other support to encourage people to go home, to resettle and grow crops again.

Photo: B. Press / UNHCR

July 1993: following widespread floods, 100 Queen's Gurkha engineers from Hong Kong flew to Nepal to help in relief operations.

July 1993: in Iraq, the ODA worked to relieve the plight of people oppressed by the dictator Saddam Hussein on two fronts – with the UN and voluntary organisations in the north and indirectly with voluntary organisations in the south.

Over the year ODA provided almost 19 million for Iraqi citizens.

September 1993: in the immediate aftermath of the Maharashtra earthquake, the ODA dispatched almost £1 million of emergency aid to the area.

February 1994: £2.5 million provided for refugees in Afghanistan, added to the £5 million already provided since April 1993.

March 1994: £2.25 million was pledged to help over a million displaced and vulnerable people in Armenia, Azerbaijan and Georgia.

April 1994: for victims of civil conflict in Tajikistan, Britain gave £1.5 million to be used for constructing shelters, providing food and better medical facilities and community health care.

The ODA is running a £10 million programme to restore basic electricity supplies in central Bosnia. ODA engineers are repairing power stations, reopening coal mines to fuel the power stations, and mending supply lines to provide electricity to local communities. Road engineers maintaining life-saving convoy routes, radio operators, fitters, telecommunicatons experts and logisticians, all paid for by British aid, have been working for UNHCR throughout Bosnia and Croatia.

Being prepared

The 1990s have been designated the International Decade for Disaster Reduction. The IDDR focuses on what governments and communities can do to minimise the damage caused by natural disasters around the world. For the past three years the ODA has devoted a small but increasing amount of its emergency aid budget to preparing for disasters and reducing their impact.

The countries which suffer most when disaster strikes are often the poorest. Many developing countries do not have the infrastructure or resources to reduce the risk from earthquakes, storms, floods, and drought. Rapid urbanisation has not helped, often creating slums with large populations, unsafe housing and poor facilities.

But with help from technical experts, local communities can do a lot to reduce the effects of natural hazards when they do strike. Fitting lightweight roofs that will not crush people if they collapse, for example, or building community shelters for protection during tropical storms are just two of the simple steps that can be taken.

In 1993/94 the ODA spent over £2 million on disaster preven-tion projects, including a Save the Children Fund 'risk-mapping' pro-gramme in Malawi which aims to indentify areas most prone to drought and an Intermediate Technology Development Group project which will help prepare Peru for earth-quakes.

In January last year one of ODA's volunteer drivers, Paul Goodall, was tragically murdered.

His death sent shock waves through all the aid organisations working Bosnia. He had worked for the 'Nomads' trucking operation in Zenica, central Bosnia, for a year and was nearing the end of his tour of duty. Ambushed by militia from a nearby mercenary camp, Paul was later shot dead on the banks of the river Bosnia. A plinth now stands where Paul Goodall fell, a tribute to his bravery and to the 20,000 other civilians killed in the crossfire of this brutal conflict. He is sorely missed.

The massive relief operation in Bosnia accounted for £52 million or nearly one third of Britain's emergency aid expenditure in 1993/4. Since the outbreak of the conflict in the former Yugoslavia in 1992, Britain has provided over £173 million, in emergency aid and through contributions to the European Community, to relieve suffering in the area.

The backbone of all ODA emergency aid activities in Bosnia over the past two years has been the convoys. The ODA's 90 trucks and over 100 drivers have delivered vital relief supplies seven days a week via several routes into Bosnia. At times aid cannot reach Sarajevo by plane, the convoys are the people's only lifeline. The ODA also manages the UNHCR ware-houses at Zagreb and Metkovic which are the main centres for distribution of relief supplies to central Bosnia.

The above is an extract from the *British Overseas Aid Annual Review 1994*. See page 39 for address details.

© *Overseas Development Administration December, 1994*

Refugees in Europe

Western European countries grant refugee status to one in ten asylum seekers, according to United Nations statistics. Between 1989 and 1993, some 171,000 asylum seekers were recognized as refugees and a further 183,000 people were allowed to stay for humanitarian reasons

◇ *Applications for asylum (1993)*
▶ *Granted refugee status/allowed to stay on humanitarian grounds*

Country	◇ Applications	▶ Granted
Holland	35,400	15,000
Germany	322,800	16,500
Norway	12,900	800
UK	22,400	12,700
Sweden	37,600	35,700
France	27,600	9,900
Denmark	14,400	2,800
Belgium	26,900	1,000
Portugal	2,100	0
Austria	4,700	1,200
Spain	12,900	1,000
Italy	1,500	100
Switzerland	24,700	4,700

Source: United Nations High Commissioner for Refugees (November 1994)   © GRAPHIC NEWS

N.B.

1. Differences in recognition rates between the asylum countries should be interpreted with care as there are no common standards for the recording, compilation and dissemination of statistics.

2. Ex-Yugoslavs, one of the largest group of asylum seekers in the last few years, are included in Swedish statistics, but mostly excluded from the statistics of other countries where they are adjudicated on a group rather than an individual basis.

3. Acceptance figures for Spain concern January to June only.

Help settling in Britain

From the Refugee Council

Many newly arrived refugees are desperate, vulnerable and disorientated. Some have been tortured. Their relatives or friends may have been killed or have disappeared. Most arrive penniless, many with nothing but the clothes they stand in.

The process of arrival and settlement in the UK is often harrowing. Fears that the Asylum & Immigration Appeals Act, which came into force in late July 1993, would have very grave consequences for asylum-seekers have proved well founded. New accelerated procedures and very tight time limits for appeals against refusals mean that some asylum seekers have to give notice and grounds of appeal against a refusal within two days, and the appeal may be heard in eight days. Together with new identification requirements, the Act has made applying for asylum difficult and extremely unnerving. There has been a drastic fall in the proportion of asylum seekers receiving Exceptional Leave to Remain. According to lawyers in the field, people who would have received this discretionary right to remain in the past are now being refused.

All arriving asylum seekers are likely to run into severe practical and emotional difficulties, as they come to terms with a society that is complex, alien, impersonal and in many ways inhospitable. A major area of worry is the long wait many must endure before they may be joined by their families.

Not only is little extra help available, but some regulations discriminate against the asylum seeker – for instance, 10 per cent of Income Support is withheld from asylum seekers awaiting a decision on their application. Housing is likely to be grim; single refugees find it almost impossible to find a good permanent home; many spend a period on the streets. The Asylum Act imposes a harsher test of homelessness on asylum seeking families and other vulnerable groups such as pregnant women or elderly people seeking housing from local authorities. Fewer and fewer places are available on English language courses; jobs – especially jobs in careers followed in the home country – are found to be out of reach; vocational training barred or difficult to obtain and health care services often unable to respond.

The first months are crucial. After the trauma of persecution and escape, the stark realities of starting a life in Britain mean refugees need all the help they can get.

Advice to the vulnerable new arrivals

The Advice and Referral team continues its work with newly arrived asylum seekers and other vulnerable groups who have made recent claims for asylum. The year has seen an increase in numbers to a total of 9,416 people of 106 nationalities.

The walk-in advice service offers a session covering immigration status, housing, benefits, health, education and employment. In addition the team offers follow-up appointments to clients, a telephone advice line, an Outreach Worker who works particularly with single parent families in bed and breakfast hotels, a Temporary Accommodation Worker vetting private rented accommodation and maintaining a daily list of reasonable accommodation, and a Police Registration worker administering refunds to people granted leave to remain as the result of an asylum application.

Legislation and procedures are changing fast, especially since the 1993 Asylum Act. This places additional demands on advisers. For instance, the asylum seekers' questionnaire on the substance of their claim must now be returned in four weeks. With housing and benefit problems alone taking at least a week to resolve, and the wait for a solicitor's appointment averaging about three weeks, most cases now start off as matters of urgency verging on crisis.

Support for Refugee Community Organisations

The Community Development Team offers advice and support to community organisations on issues such as charitable status, legal structures, equal opportunities, fundraising and management. Some of this help is given through one-to-one work and this year the team worked in this way with 60 organisations. The team prioritised new and unfunded groups and women's organisations.

The last year has also been one of getting to grips with the increasing demands from community organisations for practical help and support in finance and fundraising. As well as one-to-one consultancy, workshops covering financial planning, financial management, PAYE and book-keeping were organised. Seminars on making funding applications, and 'How to Target Funding Bodies' were also held.

The team's newsletter continues to be an important channel for providing communities with information to assist their work. The newsletter went out every six weeks and contained articles on funding opportunities, charity law, health and social security issues, implementation of the Asylum and Immigration Appeals Act and many more.

• The above is an extract from the *Refugee Council Annual Report 1994.*

On detention duty

From the the diary of a Refugee Council worker

9.05 Monday's first call is from Harwich Immigration. They have two asylum seekers from Albania, both women, aged 20 and 23. They were picked up on Saturday night and have been detained since then. They came by sea in a container and are both quite shaken. Immigration want to release them today. I take the details, and ask the usual questions: they have one small bag between them, no money, no English. They should be able to get them to us by 4 pm.

I tell him I will call back – I need to talk my colleague on reception duty. We quickly juggle priorities. She has already reserved places for two other detention cases – both single men, a Romanian and an Angolan, and the waiting room is already filling up with clients. But neither of us feel the two women should be held in a port detention centre for another night. We agree to make time for them and hope that the number of clients stays within a manageable level. I speak to the Temporary Accommodation Worker – yes he will book something for them at least for tonight as an emergency measure. I ring Harwich back to confirm that we will take them today.

9.40 The first thing I must arrange is an interpreter – not easy at such short notice. But before I can get on to this, the switchboard calls to say the Romanian and Angolan have arrived. A help group in Dover organised their release from detention on Friday, accommodated them over the weekend and put them on a bus to Victoria early this morning. I go down to the lobby to greet them. The Romanian is reasonably clothed for Britain. The Angolan has no coat. He is carrying a small plastic bag. They both look very bewildered.

I gave them as warm a welcome as possible, and usher them into the waiting area. Already it is filling up. The atmosphere of anticipation and anxiety is not unlike the check-in area at Terminal 4, but instead of clutching airline tickets people are holding on to their Home Office papers and keeping an eye hopefully on the receptionist. It is like some bizarre lottery with information, advice and accommodation as the prizes.

Luckily the Portuguese inter-preter is already here and one of my colleagues speaks Romanian, so the first major hurdle is avoided. The receptionist checks and tells me that one of the advisers will be free in about 20 minutes. The second Reception worker is deep in conver-sation with a client finding out about his DSS problem. As I leave a client from last week, an Afghan woman, greets me and asks me for help with her problem. I explain I'm on a different duty today and that she needs to talk to the receptionist.

10.00 Back in my office I check with Switchboard. Manchester Immigration want me to ring them. They want to release a pregnant Nigerian woman: do I know any agencies in the Manchester area who could help? I give them a list.

10.35 The Dover group rings again; they have two more referrals. The first one is straightforward: a Sudanese man who applied for asylum a month ago, and was assisted by us, was returned to France yesterday because he had spent two days there in transit. Like many such cases these days, the French authorities sent him straight back. Fortunately his room is still available. But the episode may well complicate his benefits claim.

The second referral is more complex: a Zairean family – mother, father and two children aged three and five. Immigration have decided to detain the husband in Rochester prison. The woman is very distraught. And she has to decide whether to stay in Dover or come to London, neither offering easy access to Rochester. In the end she opts for London: she has a cousin here somewhere, although she doesn't have an address. Her husband will be detained tonight in Dover Harbour-side detention unit and be transferred to the prison tomorrow. I need to contact a London housing authority to arrange accommodation for her, book an interpreter, write referral letters to the Housing Department and DSS. As she is now a single parent she could be referred to our Outreach Worker for follow-up visits after the initial advice session.

10.40 The Temporary Accommo-dation officer calls by. He has not yet found a place for the two Albanian women but he assures me he is on the case! I manage to book a Lingala speaker for the Zairian women. Harwich Immigration call to say that they are still doing the women's papers. It looks like the Home Office is going to send them back to Holland. They have lodged an appeal but for the moment they have to expect to report back to Immigration in 10 days. Their first DSS payment will be needed to pay the fare back to the port.

The second floor is buzzing: in their offices advisers are locked into the multiple problems and anxieties of the newly arrived: where to find a doctor, a solicitor – will I be sent back? Children from Ivory Coast and Iran are playing noisily in the corridor. The mother of the Iranian children is in tears . . .

The above is an extract from the Refugee Council Annual Report 1994.

Britain 'barring more refugees'

By Alan Travis
Home Affairs Editor

The rate at which asylum seekers are being refused entry to Britain has leapt in the past 15 months from 16 per cent to 75 per cent of all applicants, according to the Refugee Council.

Immigration lawyers say the unprecedented refusal rate marks a change in Britain's treatment of refugees with a 'culture of disbelief' towards applicants now prevalent at the Home Office.

The sharp rise in the refusal rate follows the Asylum and Immigration Appeals Act which became law in July 1993. All but a few of those refused asylum face involuntary repatriation.

The Council said many of the asylum seekers who were being rejected had fled countries in civil war or suffering from well documented abuses of human rights or breakdowns in civil order.

Since the new legislation became law, 96 per cent of Zaireans, 97 per cent of Angolans, and 84 per cent of Sri Lankan Tamils had been refused entry. Before the act over 98 per cent of Tamils were allowed to remain in the UK.

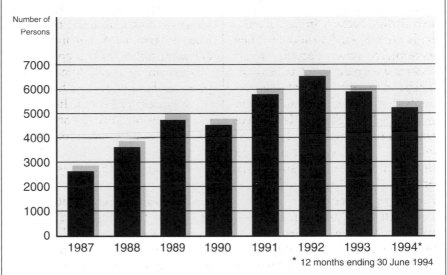

Home Office Statistics of Expulsions from UK

Number of Persons

(Bar chart showing number of persons expelled by year: 1987 ≈ 2600, 1988 ≈ 3600, 1989 ≈ 4700, 1990 ≈ 4500, 1991 ≈ 5800, 1992 ≈ 6600, 1993 ≈ 5900, 1994* ≈ 5300)

* 12 months ending 30 June 1994

Susannah Cox, of the Council, said: 'While the Act introduced a right of appeal for all asylum seekers, legal advisers note that fewer applicants than ever are successful. The Act itself limits the grounds which can be raised on appeal.

'Access to and time for legal advice has been hit by the new 'fast-track' procedures, and the doubling of the number of asylum seekers placed in prisons and detention centres.'

The latest figures for asylum applications have also risen sharply. In March last year, 42,170 were awaited a decision but by September 30 this year the figure had risen to 52,760.

The council said: 'Asylum seekers are being put in the position of having to disprove negative interpretations of their case with disproportionate emphasis being placed early on in the process on watertight, documented evidence, which is often extremely difficult to obtain from countries of origin. A claim which is not fully supported can be abruptly refused.'

The numbers held in prisons while their applications were determined had trebled since the Act, with 606 behind bars in June this year. More than 100 had been held for more than a year.

INDEX

ADDITIONAL RESOURCES

You might like to contact the following organisations for further information. Due to the increasing cost of postage, many organisations cannot respond to inquiries unless they receive a stamped, addressed envelope.

Action Aid
Hamlyn House
MacDonald Road
Archway
London, N19 5PG
Tel: 0171 281 4101

British Red Cross Society
9 Grosvenor Cresent
London, SW1X 7EJ
Tel: 0171 235 5454

CHAR (Housing Campaign for Single People)
1 – 15 Cromer Street
London, WC1H 8LSQ
Tel: 0171 833 2071

CHAS (The Catholic Housing Aid Society)
209 Old Marylebone Road
London, NW1 5QT
Tel: 0171 723 7273

Child Poverty Action Group (CPAG)
1 – 5 Bath Street
London, EC1V 9PY
Tel: 0171 253 3406

Childline
2nd Floor
Royal Mail Building
Studd Street
London, N1 0QW
Tel: 0171 239 1000

Children's Legal Centre
20 Crompton Terrace
London, N1 2UN
Tel: 0171 359 9392

Crisis
7 Whitechapel Road
London, E1 1DU
Tel: 0171 377 0489

FEANTSA
1, Rue Defacz
1050-Bruxelles
Belique
Tel: 32 2 539 66 69
Fax: 32 2 539 41 74

Immigration Aid Unit
400 Cheetham Hill Road
Manchester 8
Tel: 0161 740 7722

Joint Council of Welfare & Immigrants
115 Old Street
London EC1V 9JR
Tel: 0171 251 8706/8

National Children's Bureau
8 Wakely Street
London EC1V 7QE
Tel: 0171 843 6000

National Society for the Prevention of Cruelty to Children (NSPCC)
National Centre
42 Curtain Road
London EC2A 3NH
Tel: 0171 825 2500

NCH Action for Children
85 Highbury Park
London N5 1UD
Tel: 0171 226 2033

Oxfam
274 Banbury Road
Oxford OX2 7DZ
Tel: 01865 311 311

Refugee Action
The Offices
The Cedars
Derby DE21 4FY
Tel: 01332 833 310

Save the Children
2nd Floor
National Deposit House
1 Eastgate
Leeds LS2 7LY
Tel: 0171 703 5400

Scottish Council for Single Homeless
9 Forrest Road
Edinburgh EH1 2QH
Tel: 0131 226 4382

SHAC (The London Housing Aid Centre)
189a Old Brompton Road
London SW5 0AR
Tel: 0171 373 7276

Shelter (England)
88 Old Street
London EC1V 9HU
Tel: 0171 253 0202

Shelter (Scotland)
8 Hampton Terrace
Edinburgh EH12 5JD
Tel: 0131 313 1550

The Children's Society
Edward Rudolf House
Margery Street
London WC1X 0JL
Tel: 0171 837 4299

UNICEF
55 Lincoln's Inn Fields
London WC2A 3NB
Tel: 0171 405 5592

United Nations High Commission for Refugees (UNHCR)
7 Westminster Place Gardens
Artillery Row
London SW1P 1RL
Tel: 0171 222 3065

ACKNOWLEDGEMENTS

The publisher is grateful for permission to reproduce the following material

Chapter One: Homelessness

Homelessness in England, © Shelter, December 1994, *Singled out*, © Scottish Council for Single Homelessness, November 1994, *Homelessness*, © Central Statistical Office, Social Trends 25 1995, *Child runaways sink into crime*, © The Independent 23 November 1995, page 6, *When home is hell … kids run away*, © The Guardian, 5th October 1994, page 15, *Switching on to the young ones*, © The Guardian, 5th September 1994, page 10, *Charity for the homeless invents luncheon voucher for beggars*, © The Times, 20 February 1995, page 8, *No chance!* , © Community Care, 13-19 October 1994, page 19, *The Crisis Report's findings*, © Community Care, 13-19 October 1994, page 19, *Are you 16 or 17 and homeless?*, © CHAR Housing Campaign for Single People, 1995, *Homeless people in the European Union*, © FEANTSA, *The right to a home, the right to a future*, 1994, *Left out in the cold*, © The Guardian, 19th December, page 10, *Sleep rough and help the homeless worldwide*, © The Big Issue, January 1995 page 10, *Preventing homelessness, campaigning for change*, © Shelter, Annual Review 1993/4, *Fight to survive driven by fear and loneliness*, © The Independent, 23 November 1994, *Moving on with the times*, © The Guardian, 27th May 1994, *Doorway to a new life*, © The Telegraph Plc, London 1994, *Reasons for homelessness*, © CHAS, July 1994, *It could happen to you*, © The Tablet, 3rd December 1994.

Chapter Two: Refugees

Refugees and asylum seekers, © British Red Cross, A great tragedy of our time, © UNHCR, 1994, *Children: a right to refuge*, © Save the Children, November 1994, *Buddy system aids school to ease pain of pupils in exile*, © The Independent, 1994, *Refugee children fleeing war 'need better support'*, © The Independent, 17th October 1994, *Refugees and displaced people*, Oxfam, February 1995, *Promoting solutions*, UNHCR, February 1995, *UNHCR at a glance*, © UNHCR, *Relief and refuge*, © Overseas Development Administration, December 1994, *Help settling in Britain*, © Refugee Council, 1994, *On detention duty*, © Refugee Council, 1994, *Britain 'barring more refugees'*, © The Guardian, 1st December 1994.

Photographs and illustrations

Page 1: Shelter, page 2: Scottish Council for Single Homeless, pages 5, 22: A. Haythornthwaite / Folio Collective, page 6: N. Martin / Folio Collective, page 7: David Hoffman, pages 9, 16, 37: Ken Pyne, pages 10, 23: A. Smith / Folio Collective, page 12: CHAR, pages 14, 28: K. Fleming / Folio Collective, pages 24, 30, 31: UNHCR, page 28: Philip Wolmuth/ Panos Pictures, page 33: B. Press / UNHCR, page 34: Graphic News.

Craig Donnellan
Cambridge
May, 1995